SHOPLIFTER!

New Retail Architecture
and Brand Spaces

gestalten

PREFACE: A TIME FOR TRANSFORMATION

BY ALISON EMBREY MEDINA

Retail has been ingrained in our historical fabric for as long as human beings have been engaging in trade. What we know as stores, shops, and shopping centers began in central assembly marketplaces across the globe as souks, bazaars, mercados, tianguis, palengke, agoras, and piazzas. Like for any facet of history, change proved to be inevitable. Right now, retail is undergoing one of the fastest and most impactful evolutions in its history.

Why is this happening? Technology has made us more aware, knowledgeable, and savvy as shoppers than ever before. As a result, retailers face the challenge of not only finding and stocking goods, but also competing for relevance among e-commerce giants such as Amazon and Alibaba. It's a whole new retail world.

Contrary to what you may read in the news, traditional brick-and-mortar retail is not dead or dying. As much as 85 to 90 percent of purchases still occur inside the walls of a physical retail store, and that statistic is even higher if you include automobile sales. We are far from the retail apocalypse that many touted throughout 2017.

What has changed is the purpose of the physical store. Shops are morphing back into the meccas of community they once were. They're becoming places to seek job advice, meet up with an online fan group, take a yoga class, schedule a photography course, play a virtual reality game, or even get married. Out of necessity, retail stores are once again becoming a central place for community. It just might be the dawn of a new golden era of retail.

The Challenge: Ignite and Incite

While online retail sales grow by double digits and Amazon continues to expand its global dominance, there is a threat to physical retail that is even scarier: stagnancy and complacency. The retail marketplace has a growing number of brands answering to private-equity companies, a revolving door of CEOs and CMOs with zero vision, a demanding consumer, a real estate renaissance, a balance sheet hanging on a thin rope of a missed quarter, and a failed margin or an unwavering fear of the bottom line. At the same time, brands are expected to create tech-savvy, authentic, merchant-driven, sustainably built, design-centric shopping experiences for their customers. Needless to say, it's a lot. Let's take a step back to the outside of the store for a minute.

Store windows and visual displays were essentially the first public forms of street art. Window dressers of eras past used retail windows to make a statement, be it political or controversial, and entertain the masses. Back then, the goal was not foot traffic but differentiation. Maintaining itself as a point of differentiation is still largely at the core of what a retail window needs to be. In an age of price-comparing, internet-searching, Amazon-delivering ease, the retail world needs to reclaim a bit of controversial, jaw-dropping, heart-pounding purpose. In a climate where consumers can find anything they want in real time on the internet, it is more important than ever for a brand to stand for something. Purpose is everything.

Store windows and visual displays were essentially the first public forms of street art. Window dressers of eras past used retail windows to make a statement, be it political or controversial, and entertain the masses. Back then, the goal was not foot traffic but differentiation.

Purpose doesn't solely have to be about politics. Stand for the environment. Stand for quality. Stand for innovation. Stand for avant-garde. Stand for anarchy. Stand for comfort. Just stand for something so you don't become a stagnant, complacent retailer that packs its shelves with stuff. Be a brand that people care about, that becomes a part of your customers' lives. Be a need instead of a want. Your physical store will become like a temple for your brand that consumers love and need.

Ann Fine Patterson, a former columnist of mine who has led the brand and visual charge for top retailers like Starbucks, REI, Limited, and Macy's, once wrote that retail is like a cupcake. It's a fine balance of frosting and cake: too much frosting looks nice but doesn't tell the story and too much cake without the sweet stuff on top fails to connect emotionally with the consumer. While her analogy makes sense, it doesn't completely describe what we have seen in retail over the last 10 years or so. Many perfectly balanced cupcakes exist in retail today but they have been serving up prepackaged, stale cupcakes. The freshness is gone. The newness is missing. Too many brands have become complacent and irrelevant, and it's time to change that. Physical retailers remain at the center of shopping but they need to be doing more.

The Human Experience

A quick scan of television, radio, or print advertising will show an idealized version of yourself, whether it's a better parent, cook, dresser, coworker, or even lover. However, there's a current shift in advertising towards self-acceptance. Be yourself. You do you. We won't judge.

In the areas of beauty, fashion, fitness, health, and wellness, brands are focusing on the power of you. This spans across generations. Baby Boomers are just as into comfortable, breathable fabrics and organic, skin-toning serums as Millennials are. Focusing on your well-being, state of mind, and happiness is no longer seen as arrogant or self-indulgent but rather a sign of sound body and mind.

At a recent retail conference, Lindsay Angelo, a strategist at the yoga-inspired athletic apparel brand lululemon, explained how facets of today's new consumer directly impact the experiences lululemon creates in its retail stores. She touched upon the ideologies of mindfulness, fearlessness, empathy, and creativity, all of which are widely raising the bar for innovation and paving the way for an experience economy to emerge. But what was really fascinating is how these thoughts translate into emotion, brand relevance, and customer connection at lululemon. Angelo referenced Abraham Maslow's hierarchy of needs, a theory in psychology that includes five motivational needs, beginning with the basic

physiological need for safety, love, and esteem and leading up to self-actualization. The theory contends that once one need is fulfilled, a person is motivated to fulfill the next one. Within Maslow's hierarchy, self-actualization includes realizing personal potential, self-fulfillment, seeking personal growth, and peak experiences. According to Angelo, "The future of retail is self-actualization."

I believe she's right. When I speak about driving more experiences in brick-and-mortar retail, I'm not talking about self-checkout robots, selfie stations, information kiosks, or adding additional SKUs. I'm talking about curated moments, facets of thought, lifestyle awareness, and self-actualization messages that transform a store into a place where you can achieve sound body and mind. A place where you can do you.

Let's look at how Maslow's hierarchy applies to the typical grocery store. I'll use a recent experience of mine as an example. If the market was only fulfilling physiological needs, I would have grabbed bread and milk and been on my way. But instead, I saw giant graphics of juicy peaches and imagined how they'd be perfect in a cobbler for my cookout. I watched the fishmonger gently filet the halibut, showing off his knife skills. Then, the wine tasting sealed the deal. Not only did I leave with a fabulous rosé from Provence that made me feel incredibly fancy and worldly, but I also joined the wine club.

In a tech-driven world where we experience much of life through a lens or screen, taste is one of the few senses reserved

For some, the idea of a fully automated world becoming the norm rather than the exception is frightening. But retailers are looking for ways to better understand their customers while decreasing labor costs and boosting productivity; so if automated systems are the answer then so be it. Remember the first time you put your bank card into the ATM and feared you were about to drain your entire life savings? You may have asked yourself something like: "How could this machine possibly be as good/reliable/efficient as my trusty bank teller?" But then you discovered that ATMs work just fine and have since adopted them as a way of life. What about your first experience using a self-checkout kiosk at your local Home Depot? Did your thought process go something like this: "How in the world are they going to let me walk out of the store with all of these paint cans without checking my receipt?" I'm guessing you made it through the doors just fine.

Fast forward to today's world, where you can get pizza delivered to your front door by giving Alexa one command. Of course, retail will become even more automated because our lives have become increasingly automated. At last year's National Retail Federation Retail's BIG Show, a tradeshow that focuses on retail technologies, I saw scanning wands from NCR that will enable customers to check themselves out as they walk through the aisles. I met Pepper, the humanoid robot from Aldebaran Robotics and SoftBank, a personal shopper that can read human emotion and help you select the perfect outfit. And at the Intel booth, I discovered Sheima Seki, a computer that knits 3-D custom sweaters and the ShopperMX InContext virtual reality solution, which lets retail associates planogram their store aisles using goggles and virtual wands that allow you to supersize cereal boxes. "With technology like robots and artificial intelligence to free up employees, every aspect of the store and supply chain will allow retail employees to better focus on the customer and improve the store's performance," said Brian Krzanich, CEO of Intel, in an editorial published last year.

From virtual reality goggles and magic mirrors to robots that walk on their own, the sheer pace at which technology is advancing is astounding. There is talk of smart laundry rooms that reorder your detergent when it gets below a certain level and smart refrigerators that essentially restock themselves by mail order or in-store pickup when staple items are nearly gone. I've heard buzz about RFID-enabled dressing rooms that send the item you've just tried on directly to your house in another color, as well as beacons driven by LED lighting that can track movement and traffic patterns in stores.

I recently experienced IBM's Watson cognitive computing technology firsthand. The idea behind the AI is simple: it asks questions like an associate would inside a store, to do a better

wholly for in-person interaction. As a result, we are starting to see the foodie revolution take over in every category of retail, not just the channels you would expect. For example, it's not uncommon these days to have a whisky tasting at the Gant Rugger clothing store in Brooklyn or a soda fountain built into the architecture at the Warby Parker location in Detroit. Ralph Lauren and Tommy Bahama continue to open branded restaurants, and Tom's Shoes and Moleskine just entered the coffee business with hybrid retail/coffeehouse concepts. Food halls are popping up in every major U.S. city and reversing the traditional retail model of "come for the shopping, stay for the food," to "come for the food, stay for the shopping." It's a whole new gastro-focused world.

Retail is an industry prime for innovation, and bringing in food, wellness, and personal moments will be key to connecting with consumers in the future.

Technology and the Connected Store

Automation is one of the buzzwords you'll be hearing a lot in retail. Expect to see more self-checkouts, self-scanning, chatbots, artificial intelligence (AI), and robotic customer service this year and beyond. And let's not forget about virtual reality (VR). Chances are you will put on a VR headset at some point in the near future and experience the hype, or play an augmented reality app on your phone, possibly even tied to your retail shopping experience. It's all coming.

"With technology like robots and artificial intelligence to free up employees, every aspect of the store and supply chain will allow retail employees to better focus on the customer and improve the store's performance."

Stand for the environment. Stand for quality. Stand for innovation. Stand for avant-garde. Stand for anarchy. Stand for comfort. Just stand for something so you don't become a stagnant, complacent retailer that packs its shelves with stuff. Be a brand that people care about.

job of suggesting items that fulfill a specific need, desire, or cater to style. By offering a more engaging, intuitive, and relevant experience for the shopper, it ultimately aids in purchase decision. I had the opportunity to test out the new North Face personal intelligent shopper in beta and I have to say it really works. After asking specific questions about my needs for a jacket, which included location, temperature, climate/weather expectations, and personal style, the program was able to recommend three jackets that should suit my needs and style, all in gorgeous, high-definition 3-D visuals. And you know what? It was right on the money and I wound up purchasing one of the recommendations.

Amid all of these evolving technologies and online conveniences, we still have an overwhelming need to connect. It's why people who work from home sometimes camp out at coffee shops for the day. It's why stay-at-home moms arrange play dates. It's why we choose to have a quick sandwich and a nightcap at the hotel bar among other business travelers instead of ordering room service. The desire for human connection is still a driver for the social interactions we choose, and shopping is certainly still one of them.

We are inherently sensory- and tactile-driven creatures; seeing, touching, and trying on merchandise is still cited as the number-one reason to shop in-store. Retailers can't be afraid to let shoppers evoke that power of touch and experience in their stores, and to make those moments as sensorial and experiential as possible.

Conclusion: The Future Is Flexible

The future of retail is a story of omnipresence: in stores, online, on phones, via conversational commerce such as chatbots, Alexa, Google Home, and more. The challenge for brands will be to make sure every touchpoint operates seamlessly while also remaining true to the brand.

In today's retail marketplace, there is an overarching sense of immediacy prevalent in every consumer interaction. I call this the now-ness of retail. Shoppers don't care about what happened yesterday, last week, or last month in your store. They want to engage in the experience in this moment.

With customers always expecting fresh and new, surprise and delight with each shopping experience, how can retailers keep brick-and-mortar stores relevant? The age-old nursery rhyme "Jack Be Nimble" comes to mind when thinking about the flexibility, speed, and immediacy necessary in retail today. As the rhyme goes: "Jack be nimble, Jack be quick, Jack jump over the candlestick." Back in the mid-nineteenth century, said to be the origin of this particular rhyme, jumping over the candle without

extinguishing the flame was a sign of good luck and a vague way of seeing into the future. The idea that speed, agility, nimbleness, and efficiency can propel you into a more logical future is one that retailers should live by.

When anyone asks me what trends I see for retail now and in the future, I swiftly and confidently say flexibility. How can retailers create sticky, brand-saturated moments of curation for customers, while also delivering the speed and agile efficiency they crave? Women's athletic apparel brand Oiselle, which recently opened its first-ever physical store in Seattle, is doing a great job of this. The up-and-coming online brand opened its location with nimbleness at the core of its store design. Aptly named The Gathering Place, the store features floor fixtures engineered on a winch system that allows store associates to literally lift the fixtures, merchandise and all, up to the ceiling for a quick turnaround. This enables the retailer to use its floor space for more than just a store. It can be a community center to meet customers, host workshops, run fitness classes—all allowing the brand to be a better steward of its overall ethos. Oiselle has created a place to not just come and shop, but to come and be.

In the coming year, it's important for retailers to approach every project, practice, and presentation with speed and ability. To go back to the candlestick metaphor, remember to size up the candlestick before taking the leap. Be nimble and quick enough to always be ready to jump forward into the future—just make sure to clear the flame. <

SERGIO ROSSI Boutique

Milan-based designer CRISTINA CELESTINO created a salon-style boutique to celebrate the launch of Sergio Rossi's new sr1 line. Combining her trademark contemporary flair with an ironic femininity, she has filled the brand's Paris shop with objects to study, admire, and purchase.

Established in Milan in 1966, Sergio Rossi is renowned for the elegance, femininity, and craftsmanship of its handmade shoes. For the launch of its 2017 sr1 collection in Paris, the brand enlisted Italian designer Cristina Celestino to create a fitting boutique. The first thing you'll notice about Celestino's design is that the shoes are displayed sparingly, as if part of a private collection. Instantly, you are made aware of the brand's exclusivity. Flanked by brightly lit textured wood wall displays, Celestino's seductive salon is rich with Milanese-inspired hues: soft nude and chalk tones punctuated with amaranth and pine green. In a stroke of ironic genius, her custom-designed furniture takes inspiration from the shoes themselves, like low-level nabuk-upholstered display stands and a sofa with legs in the shape of the sr1 heel. In a nod to the company's heritage, a freestanding mirror recalls the days of the artisan atelier. Finishing touches range from richly figured marbles to soft carpeting and quirky, textured walls. These elements serve as Celestino's personal interpretation of the harmonious shapes and textures of Serigo Rossi's shoes. <

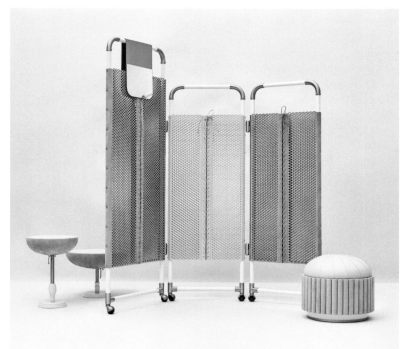

The store is as much a living room as a boutique; Celestino custom-designed the furniture for this space. An elegant sofa takes center stage—reflected in the freestanding mirror—and small coffee tables double as display stands.

ARKET Flagship Store

Creative director ULRIKA BERNHARDTZ gambles with an all-gray palette for the Copenhagen branch of lifestyle store Arket, set in a historical townhouse that once served as the headquarters of the Royal Danish Mail.

Arket means "sheet of paper" in Swedish and is the latest addition to the H&M group's bulging portfolio. The brand is built on three core concepts: archives, archetypes, and the market. Here, Bernhardtz uses the first of these—archives—as her primary point of inspiration, specifically the layout of historical record offices. Given that this Copenhagen townhouse once housed an archive, it's a fitting approach to take for both the building and the brand. Bernhardtz's creation features its own archive system, which sees walls lined with shelves and pigeonholes. The floor space is occupied by high tables that have been modeled on desks. The scheme is entirely gray in color, with a range of materials creating depths of shade and texture—larch, birch, ash, stainless steel, aluminum, and rubber among them. The effect is a neutral backdrop against which the wares on display surely remain the focal point. <

Shelving with numerous pigeonholes and display units that resemble filing drawers offer hints of the building's previous use as a historical archive facility. The flat gray backdrop allows the colors of Arket's clothing to pop.

ARKET Flagship Store

GIGI VERDE Store

Bathed in natural light and awash with neutral colors, SIDES CORE'S interior design for the Gigi Verde florist's store has the tranquility of a Japanese garden. Center stage stands a sculptural, tree-wrapped arch.

Grace and serenity are the two words that readily spring to mind when entering the Gigi Verde florist's store in Japan's cosmopolitan city of Kobe. The interior design is the work of Osaka-based Sides Core, an architectural outfit much praised for its minimalist creations. Inside, the space is sparse, its main feature a lean, gracious metal arch that spans its width. Fixed at each end to a block of rough-hewn wood, the arch can take a number of positions in the store, defining new spaces at the whim of its owne. Sides Core has kept the rest of the store neutral, deliberately preserving the original pockmarked concrete floor and casting panels for cabinets in raw concrete, so leaving the flowers to speak for themselves. Artfully arranged, the blooms create a sculptural focal point, their colors, textures, and tones lending verdant dynanism to the scene. And all is not static here. At the back of the store stands a hip-height partition behind which the florist can work—visible to passersby, without the clutter of her activity encroaching on the otherwise tranquil setting. <

GIGI VERDE Store, Kobe

REDVALENTINO Flagship Store

Parisian architect and designer India Mahdavi captures the romantic-eccentric spirit of REDValentino in her creation for a flagship store in London, setting the brand's products within a dreamy landscape that is vibrant, sensuous, and feminine.

Behind a bold brass-and-glass façade lies an enchanting space created by Parisian architect and designer India Mahdavi in celebration of REDValentino's arrival on London's prestigious Sloane Street in 2016. Dubbed the little sister of Valentino's fashion label, RED is quirky and feminine, youthful and dynamic. Launched in 2004, RED stands for romantic eccentric design, and no three words better summarize Mahdavi's interpretation of the style. Mahdavi created a series of visually exciting, tactile spaces where brass mixes with velvet on funky terrazzo flooring in a harmonious blend of soft pink and ocher hues. Pairs of shoes trip down a flight of plush stairs, and accessories are displayed on outsized Rubik's Cubes and truncated fluted columns as if in some dreamy wonderland. Wall-to-wall brass racks allow for easy browsing, with plenty of mirrors in which to admire the latest styles. Sensuous and feminine, curves rule the day in the soft forms of Mahdavi's Charlotte chairs and voluptuous, tiled columns. <

ARTEDOMUS Showroom

For Casa Artedomus, Sydney design outfit THE STELLA COLLECTIVE and THOMAS COWARD teamed up to transform a traditional showroom into a three-dimensional mood board for architects, interior designers, and homeowners.

Founded in 1985, Artedomus is Australia's leading supplier of high-quality stone and tiling materials. Sourcing products from around the globe, the company boasts an impressive range of marbles, limestones, and ceramics, as well as bathware and furniture. Because they are made from natural materials, Artedomus's wares are predominantly black, white, gray, and beige, albeit with a beautiful range of tones and exquisite figuring. When The Stella Collective and Thomas Coward were brought in to develop a prestigious Sydney showroom for the brand, designer Hana Hakim and Thomas Coward immediately drew on the concept of creating room sets inspired by the black-and-white movies of Hollywood's Golden Age. Wares are arranged to create the look of a real bathroom or dining room, complete with curtains, screens, and even houseplants. A tour through the store leaves customers feeling like they are in a dream home rather than a showroom. Since the products are heavy, custom displays such as pedestals, screens, and plinths, in classical designs, can easily be rearranged to create different room sets within the space. <

The interior design scheme is at one with the store's wares, so much so that it relies on a very limited color palette. There are no bold prime colors or neons here, simply the subtle grays and soft browns of nature's most precious rocks and stones, punctuated with a rich basalt black.

KADEWE Women's Floor

Strong graphic lines and monochrome colors meet feminine luxury and comfort in India Mahdavi's lavish creation for the women's floor of KaDeWe in Berlin. Her Bauhaus-inspired design makes bold use of geometric forms, contrasting the utilitarian with the intimate.

Europe's second-largest department store, KaDeWe (Kaufhaus des Westens) lies in the shopping district of what, for half a century, was West Berlin. Following a refurbishment of the entire store by Dutch architect Rem Koolhaas, India Mahdavi was commissioned to design a new look for the women's floor. Taking cues from Berlin's history and culture, and maximizing the vast floor space at her disposal, Mahdavi made bold use of the geometry and architectural motifs associated with the Bauhaus movement of the 1930s. Regimented strips of marble in black, white, and gray pave the floor, guiding customers from one clothing brand to the next. The same graphic element gives shape to arches and pillars at entrances and doorways. The strong architectural details and monochrome colors lend a distinct masculinity to the design as a counterpoint to the femininity of the clothing. The look is softened by the roundness of the shapes displayed, the luxury of brass fittings, and baby pink hues throughout, further complementing the women's fashion on display. <

RETAIL'S FUTURE IS PHYSICAL

ALISON EMBREY MEDINA—Editor in Chief & Associate Publisher, design:retail magazine

Today's news headlines would have you believing online shopping is winning, that traditional retail is dying and that "the great retail apocalypse" is upon us. In truth, around 90 percent of purchases still occur inside the walls of a physical retail store. It's not an apocalypse we are seeing, it's a metamorphosis. Retail is transforming to adapt to a faster, more agile, and more efficient future. It has to.

Retail is experiencing an epic metamorphosis. Legacy retailers have to quickly figure out how to be cool again, while sleek and nimble e-commerce brands swoop in and steal market share—and customer loyalty. One commonality? From trusted brands to pure-play start-ups, all retailers have recentered their focus on the physical store. They have to because whether brands are targeting Baby Boomers or Gen Z consumers, experience is everything.

While news headlines have played up a lovely battle of online versus brick-and-mortar, with physical retail dying a slow and painful death, the fact is that 85–90 percent of purchases still happen inside the walls of a physical store. But since uncertainty causes chaos, the storyline of the day is that retail is dying. I believe this is fundamentally untrue.

Roger Wade, founder of the innovative British pop-up mall Boxpark, has said that shopping online is about as thrilling as "watching fireworks on TV." Have you ever been to a live fireworks show? If you have, you can close your eyes right now and smell the smoke, hear the echo of the explosion as the boom reverberates off nearby buildings, see the powerful visual of the night sky all lit up, and watch the colorful embers slowly trickle down toward land. It's an exhilarating, sensorial experience. In contrast, watching fireworks on TV is incredibly boring because it eviscerates the moments that make the experience memorable. Similarly, online brands cannot generate the excitement that physical stores can because on the web every brand is inherently one-dimensional.

In the expectation economy we live in today, consumers demand that the brands they love constantly make their lives easier or better; otherwise it's not worth their time. Retail today must be more than just a place that sells stuff; it has to be a part of its customers' lives. The retailers that are closing doors are the ones that have failed to innovate in a period of disruption. Innovation today has to be a constant cycle, a new way of life.

A Metamorphosis

We read headline after headline about the doom and gloom of the retail apocalypse, as if some singular event has defined the fate of all stores.

Let's set something straight. An apocalypse is "an event involving destruction or damage on an awesome or catastrophic scale." By this definition, there is no retail apocalypse. Despite the recurrence of store closures and bankruptcies, there is another wave of value, off-price, luxury, and start-up retailers that are opening stores at what some might call an accelerated pace. Retailers are renovating, innovating, and trying new things daily.

According to global research and advisory firm IHL Group, for every one retail company that is closing its doors, there are 2.7 companies that are opening stores. "The negative narrative that has been out there about the death of retail is patently false," says Greg Buzek, founder and president of IHL Group. "The so-called 'retail apocalypse' makes for a great headline, but it is simply not true. Over 4,000 more stores are opening than closing among big chains, and when smaller retailers are included, the net gain is well over 10,000 new stores ... Through the first seven months of the year (2017), retail sales in the U.S. are up $121.6 billion, an amount roughly equivalent to the total annual retail sales of the Netherlands."

A more appropriate term for the current state of retail, in my humble opinion, is a metamorphosis: "A change of the form or nature of a thing or person into a completely different one, by natural or supernatural means."

Some of us are still caterpillars, slow, steady, and hopelessly full of the expectation of growth and change. We are lazily sunning ourselves on the tree branch, crawling toward the edge of the leaves, hoping something or someone will figure out how to make us fly before we get to the end. Many caterpillars have fallen out of the tree. More will fall. Some of us have laboriously begun wrapping the cocoon, hanging on for dear life, brainstorming, ideating, and wondering what beautiful type of butterfly will emerge on the other side. We are eager and ready for change, but we are not quite in control of it. And some are already flying high, never looking back. They have taken the giant leap and are moving full-steam ahead into a lighter, brighter, and much, much faster future.

What is happening in retail right now is not an apocalypse, but one of science's most golden rules: natural selection. Adapt or die. Survival of the fittest. Darwin did not use the term "fittest" to mean the fastest, strongest, or smartest. "Fittest," in his view, meant the one "best suited for the immediate environment."

Blame Amazon. Blame the demanding consumer. Blame venture capital. Blame private equity. Blame Donald Trump's tweets. There is no one single apocalyptic source here. It's the natural retail evolution

that those who adapt to "the immediate environment" of today's customer mindset will, in fact, survive. Even thrive.

Focus on the Store

Retail sales have been growing at almost four percent annually since 2010. In the United States, we have seen an uptick in new retail construction, retail rents, and occupancy rates. We are also seeing a decline in foot traffic, sales, and productivity. So what's the problem? Market share. New competitors every day, coming from every direction. Many of today's retailers are over-stored, in a landscape that is already over-malled. So naturally, a general "right-sizing" is happening. To boost foot traffic, shopping center landlords are dipping into alternate lease deals that attract footfall, such as food venues and entertainment destinations. Co-working spaces are also popping up left and right on major shopping thoroughfares, targeting the freelancer or entrepreneurial start-up that needs a home on a rental basis.

Smart legacy retailers are closing some of their stores that aren't pulling weight and instead investing heavily in new concepts. For example, Nordstrom is investing major capital into opening what are expected to be two pull-out-all-the-stops stores in Manhattan in the next two years. The retailer is simultaneously opening a new concept called Nordstrom Local in Los Angeles, which offers no backstock and helps facilitate online ordering and fulfillment. The Local concept also offers experiential service offerings like buy online, pick up in store (BOPUS) and curbside pickup, same-day delivery, complimentary personal stylists and alterations, a nail bar, and a juice bar.

A trend fueled by the fast growth of brands like Warby Parker and Bonobos,

While news headlines have played up a lovely battle of online versus brick-and-mortar, with physical retail dying a slow and painful death, the fact is that 85–90 percent of purchases still happen inside the walls of a physical store.

How do we think ahead to a future that will be more agile, nimble, and with even more heightened expectations than our consumers are already demanding? The answer for many retailers is to start thinking like a start-up.

more and more e-commerce brands are setting up physical stores, including Indochino, Rent the Runway, Blue Nile, Casper, Gilt, Birchbox, and Harry's. Not only does this instantly plant a stake in the local market's retail makeup, opening a store also typically ensures a sharp spike in online sales in that market. The physical store becomes a literal billboard for the brand. "We were telling ourselves that the Bonobos experience was better because it was online only," said Andy Dunn, CEO of Bonobos, at the 2016 Shoptalk conference. "Once we put a fitting room in our lobby, we realized we were wrong."

Retailers are dipping further into the pop-up business, even making them part of the core strategy for many brands. The pop-up industry was valued at $50 billion in 2016, and it is growing. As long-term massive real estate buildout is less prevalent, retailers are looking to be more adaptive to short-term experiments and other inventive ideas. Canadian bank retailer Desjardins has launched the Mobile Branch, which is basically a mobile ATM unit that can drive up to any location and offer quick and easy money access. When opening its latest London flagship, yoga retailer Lululemon branded a traditional British double-decker bus as a full-fledged mobile meditation studio. Dubbed "Meditation Om the Move," the two-story mobile unit offered headphone-guided meditation sessions while maneuvering the crowded, hectic streets of London. This concept of rogue retailing will continue, as brands and retailers look for inventive, captivating ways to connect with their customers.

Think Like a Start-Up

What if someone told you and your team that you had the ability to change the course of retail as we know it today? What would you do? I recently met with the leader of an innovation team for a global retailer and asked him what his job looked like. His task is to sit down with his five-person team and say, "We have

$20 million and need to build a store that will open 15 years from now. Go." What will that store look like? What functionality will it have? How will it service its customers? Not the store of tomorrow, but the store of tomorrow's tomorrow.

How do we think ahead to a future that will be more agile, nimble, and with even more heightened expectations than our consumers are already demanding? The answer for many retailers is to stop thinking like an arcadian business that has done the same thing the same way for the last 50 to 100 years and to start thinking like a start-up. Let's take a look at the current back-and-forth balance scale going on between Amazon and Walmart: Amazon has the top of the market and is gaining ground in the middle—more than half of U.S. households will be Amazon Prime members by year-end. Walmart comfortably has the bottom of the market and is steadily gaining traction upward. In the middle, the battle is no longer on price but on speed. How fast can these retailers service me? The last mile becomes the last block becomes the last doorstep.

For Amazon, brick-and-mortar retail is strategically essential. The company has firmly put a stake in physical retail ground with Amazon Bookstores, Amazon-Fresh Pickup Points, and Amazon Go convenience stores, where payments are handled through Prime accounts and the need for cashiers is eliminated. On top of that, the acquisition of Whole Foods Market earlier this year gave the company nearly 500 more physical distribution points. And a new partnership with Kohl's will launch in-store Amazon shops that will enable customers to return online Amazon purchases to a physical location, eliminating one of Amazon's biggest pain points.

Meanwhile, Walmart, the world's largest brick-and-mortar retailer, has been steadily planting roots in its e-commerce game. Since purchasing Jet in 2016, the retailer has been buying up e-commerce brands that inevitably up its cool factor.

Bonobos, Moosejaw, and Modcloth are now part of the Walmart family, delivering hip, fresh fashion to your front door. A recent Jet pop-up at STORY in New York also helped promote its delivery of fresh groceries in the area. Walmart has also launched Store No. 8, an innovation incubator where the company can test new technologies and entrepreneurial start-up brands and implement them into the Walmart ecosystem where they see fit.

This does not sound like two retailers sitting idly by and waiting for the future to happen. If you can't be a start-up, think like a start-up. The future is now.

Finessing Technology

Many retailers are grappling with what to do next, and landing on quick-fix technology installs to try to reach the connected consumer in their stores. The interesting thing about in-store technology is that it can actually drive disengagement if it is unintuitive, doesn't support the customer journey, or creates a barrier between the person and the purchase. In a recent interview, Jonathan Chippindale, CEO of creative technology agency Holition, takes a jab at retailers putting iPads in-store as a means of seamless retail or bridging the offline/online gap. "When customers are walking into a real store and looking straight at an iPad, rather than the store, they aren't getting the full experience," Chippindale says. "Analogously, it's a bit like standing in front of Niagara Falls looking at a postcard of Niagara Falls—making something 3-D and multisensory into something far flatter."

Augmented reality and virtual reality (AR/VR) are popping up in retail stores left and right, acting as an immersive portal that transplants customers to another time and place while in-store. This summer, Topshop offered a VR waterslide experience that simultaneously allowed shoppers to zoom around Oxford Street on a virtual waterslide while also promoting its summer swim campaign. Lowe's is currently testing AR technology that would serve as a navigation device throughout the store, helping customers find the products they

are looking for by using their phone as a virtual map overlaid on real-time location. According to the *Harvard Business Review* (September 2016), some projections put AR/VR investment in retail at close to $30 billion by 2020, from virtually nothing as recently as two years ago.

In the near future, we are going to continue to see a rise in self-checkouts, self-scanning, chatbots, and robotic customer service assistants. These technologies are inevitably helping retailers become more efficient and streamlined in their customer service capabilities. It's

easier than ever to order something from your living room sofa and the rise of intelligent personal assistants like Alexa, Siri, and Google Home, voice commerce, or conversational commerce might be just the beginning. Accenture Research finds that 38 percent of Millennials are willing to try voice-activated ordering, and 10 percent have already used it.

Chatbots are also trickling into the mainstream. With H&M's Kik chatbot, a

What is happening in retail right now is not an apocalypse, but one of science's most golden rules: natural selection.

customer tells the bot what they are looking for, and it will build an outfit for them based on personal preferences. Sephora's Virtual Artist has a color match application where you can actually take a picture of any lipstick color, and the bot will show you the closest shade Sephora offers. You can then upload a picture of yourself, and the shade will be applied over your lips. Taco Bell's TacoBot offers an order-ahead service that has gained the fast-food retailer a 20 percent increase in average ticket, versus just coming in the store.

Automation will be a large part of retail's future. Fully automated stores already exist and deploying robots in-store seems to be only a matter of time. In fact, robots are already here. Cafe X in San Francisco's Metreon shopping center features robotic-arm baristas that prepare the perfect cup of espresso. At Zume Pizza in Silicon Valley, pizzas are made on an automated assembly line, then cooked in ovens in the back of delivery trucks while en route to their destination. Talk about a fresh-out-of-the-oven delivery service. At The Tipsy Robot in Las Vegas, patrons order drinks on iPads and then pick them up from robotic bartenders.

The Uberization of retail is only beginning. The Moby Mart, in beta testing in Shanghai, is a 24-hour self-driving store that operates with no human staff and comes right to your pinpointed GPS location, just like Uber. It runs on solar power with a mission of making grocery shopping environmentally friendly, easy to access, and cheaper to operate. It's a whole new automated world.

Retail is undergoing an extreme metamorphosis. Despite many closings and bankruptcies, newness and innovation is rising to the top. Amazon is leading the pack. If you are not paying attention to what this giant is doing, then you are sleeping under retail's biggest rock. But they are not the only ones innovating. From Starbucks to Sephora, Walmart to Aldi, the retail industry is full to the brim with brands undergoing a beautiful awakening. Who will the next butterfly be? Will you be next to find your wings? <

BERLUTI Illustrated Shop Windows

To bring Berluti's 2015 menswear line to life, Spanish illustrator JORGE LAWERTA took inspiration from the surrealist game known as exquisite corpse and presented the Berluti as a collection of portraits that combined two-dimensional illustrations with the brand's latest clothing and accessories.

A subsidiary of the luxury fashion collective LVMH, Berluti has been crafting men's boots and shoes for well over a century. Originally founded by Italian designer Alessandro Berluti and headquartered in Paris, the brand is no stranger to design flair and innovation. Known for its avant-garde designs and unique fabrics that include calfskin, alligator skin, and kangaroo leather, the brand displayed its penchant for the less ordinary when it commissioned Jorge Lawerta to design its window displays in 2015. The Spanish artist drew inspiration from the surrealist game of exquisite corpse, in which artists take turns adding elements to a collaborative drawing without knowing what has been created before. By combining illustration with Berluti's wares, Lawerta created surreal vignettes of the Berluti man in a range of guises that included a rocker, a tattooed sailor, a skater, a biker, a weightlifter, and a man wearing nothing more than his underwear. <

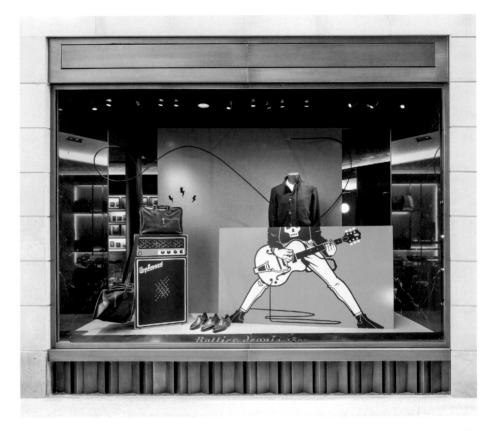

NORDSTROM Pop In

At its headquarters in Seattle, the Nordstrom department store provides novel retail space for a host of global brands with their Pop In Shop concept that showcases an exclusive range of merchandise for a limited time.

Launched as a shop-in-shop initiative, each Pop In Shop installation and product mix receives a 4- to 12-week run and is curated by Olivia Kim, Nordstrom's vice president of creative projects. The limited time-frame is key, being just long enough for the pop-up to draw the city's fashionistas without losing its edge. The concept creates a constant buzz among store visitors and in some cases offers a one-time opportu-

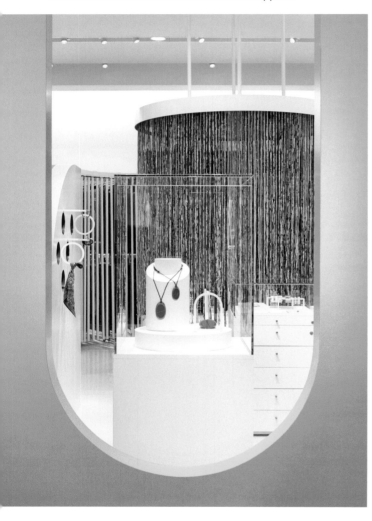

nity to sample the limited-edition items. It also allows prestigious brands to test the market in a temporary, low-risk setting. Last but not least, Nordstrom benefits from the impact of an ever-changing display, which inevitably increases foot traffic. With less emphasis on developing a theme that changes with the seasons or needs to accommodate a more diverse range of goods, this is the designer's chance to wow the customer with innovative displays and creative use of floor space. And given the fact that they are often created by some of the world's most innovative interior designers, the results can be truly dazzling, as demonstrated by an installation for Hermès by British designers from StoreyStudio. <

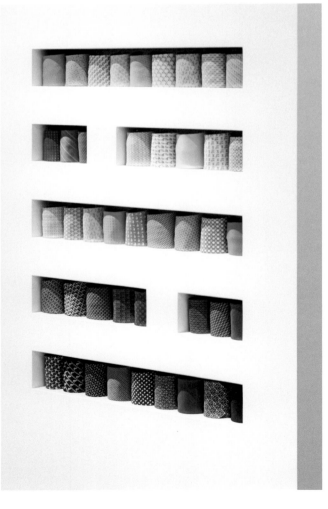

The playful, "please touch" vibe of the Hermès Pop In Shop is best summed up in its towering silk room. Hundreds of vibrantly colored strands of silk form a circular curtain wall that invites customers to walk right through.

COS Pop-Up Mobile Store

The pop-up shop concept goes mobile with CHMARA.ROSINKE's fun-meets-functional design for the urban-minded COS fashion label. Packed exquisitely neatly into a pinewood box on wheels, the store takes to the seaside streets of Brighton in the United Kingdom.

Part of the H&M group, leaders of affordable quality fashionwear, the COS label prides itself on its modern, functional, and considered design. So when Vienna-based conceptual design studio chmara. rosinke developed a pop-up store for the brand, there could literally not have been a better vehicle for pedaling their wares than this mobile cart. Built from sturdy solid pine, the wheelbarrow-like cart evolves from a compact box to a miniature clothing store in a matter of minutes, complete with a hanging rack, pull-out drawers, a mirror, stools, and plenty storage. The simple, functional aspect of the design reflects that of the clothing line it represents. Initially designed for touring the streets of the hip seaside town of Brighton, the store draws attention wherever it goes. And at the end of the day, everything is simply collapsed, packed, and rolled away. No need to lock up. <

COCA-COLA Pavilion

A dazzling burst of effervescent bubbles took center stage at MARKO BRAJOVIC's immersive installation for Coca-Cola, created to celebrate the 2016 Olympics in Rio de Janeiro, Brazil.

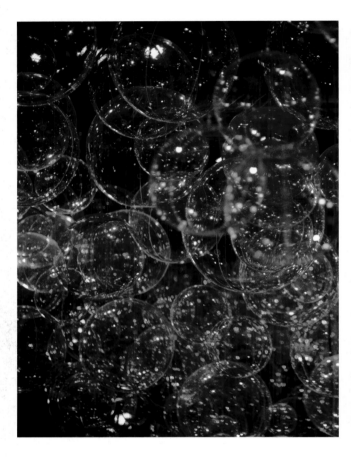

Housed in a warehouse in a revitalized Rio de Janeiro neighborhood, the Parada Coca-Cola offered visitors a multisensorial experience that merged the freshness and vitality of the beloved brand with the energy of the Olympics. The immersive installation culminated in the center of the space where a gilded, seven-meter-wide bar was showered in more than 500 translucent acrylic spheres that mimicked sparkling bubbles. The entire experience was free and included an ice-cold Coke on arrival. Visitors could take selfies with the Olympic torch, pose for a 360-degree photo, and play a real-time dance game that allowed them to post their results on Facebook within seconds. Created by Brazilian firm Atelier Marko Brajovic, the large-scale exhibition design perfectly catered to the instant gratification needs of today's social media obsessed. Screens on surrounding walls displayed Olympic footage interspersed with music videos and branded ads that ensured there was never a dull moment. <

THE PERMANENT IMPERMANENCE OF POP-UP RETAIL

ALISON EMBREY MEDINA—Editor in Chief & Associate Publisher, design:retail magazine

With retail changing as fast as it must to keep up with today's consumer mindset, retailers are becoming more and more gun-shy about signing long-term real estate deals. A culture of experimentation and trial prototyping has emerged, giving way to more agile, temporary means of concept exploration. Enter the age of pop-up retail, and the effect nomadic retail is having on retailers and brands the world over.

"Being temporary doesn't make something matter any less, because the point isn't for how long, the point is that it happened."
— Robyn Schneider, Extraordinary Means

Whether a traditional retail lease lasts 20 years, as was the average back in the 1990s, or five years, as is typical today, there is an impermanence to retail that does not exist in other industries. In retail, all good things must come to an end. As any store window designer or visual merchandiser will tell you, the fleeting nature of retail is what makes it so beautiful. Everything is built to be taken down someday—whether in three days or three decades.

Enter the world of pop-up retail, where temporary and fleeting have become the new normal. The pop-up phenomenon has been on the rise for the past decade, fueled largely during the recession of the last half of the 2000s. An abundance of available retail real estate, powered by empty storefronts and extremely low lease rates, made an already abundant pop-up retail market soar into overdrive. Now in 2017 and looking ahead, the trend is not softening: long-term massive real estate rollouts are less prevalent in today's retail market, as retailers have embraced a more adaptive, flexible, and short-term approach to experiments and brand activations.

A go-to marketing strategy for many retailers and brands, the pop-up industry has been valued as high as $50 billion. From start-ups and young e-commerce brands looking to establish a brick-and-mortar presence to legacy global brands attempting to test a new regional market or launch a new product or category, pop-up retail has become mainstream. Some might even call it a strategic necessity in today's rapidly changing retail climate.

And shoppers have bought in too. According to a survey by PopUp Republic, 61 percent of shoppers list seasonal products as the main reason to shop at a pop-up store. And we're not just talking about Christmas shopping here. Think Halloween costume pop-ups, summer swim- and sunwear shops, back-to-school fashion and supply shops—the possibilities are endless. But there are other reasons pop-ups are attractive to shoppers, according to the PopUp Republic poll:

– Unique services/products (39 percent)
– Localized assortments (36 percent)
– Optimal pricing (34 percent)
– Convenience (33 percent)
– A fun experience (30 percent)

In an age where declining store traffic is the order of the day, retailers and brands are finding new, inventive means of taking the brand to the people, versus waiting for the people to come to it.

"The great thing about pop-ups that we find all across the board—whether it's a pop-up store, pop-up restaurant, or event—is that they have this 'fear of missing out' (FOMO) quality to them," says Jeremy Baras, CEO of PopUp Republic. "Customers are attracted to exclusivity. They're attracted to a 'here today, gone tomorrow' type of concept." Creating that "limited time only" urgency resonates with the FOMO consumer—"If I don't go check out the Museum of Ice Cream, I'll never be able to Instagram a selfie in the pool of sprinkles!"

In a consumer world where flash mobs are a thing and social media can gain instant viral marketing effectiveness, pop-ups are fueling a whole new selfie-powered world. We are seeing experimentation flourish in cities across the globe, with temporary storefronts and nomadic retail presences giving retail the tools it needs to be young and free, to open up to new customer bases, regional markets, and demographics. In today's ADD-fueled consumer marketplace, the real question might be: why wouldn't a retailer jump on board?

Try Before You Buy

Getting the real estate game correct is one of the trickiest parts of the retail equation. We do very well in New York, but will Miami's consumers respond as favorably? Here's where pop-ups can solve the puzzle quickly and efficiently. Throw up a shop and try it out before signing the dotted line on that five-year lease.

In response to the prevalence of temporary retail, new marketplaces have emerged that facilitate the pop-up storefront experience with ease. One such website, called Appear Here, has been called the "Airbnb for commercial real estate." The site houses thousands of pop-up shops, retail rentals, and venues for hire. Brands can find and book short-term retail space in three global cities: London, Paris, and New York. This includes locations on prime shopping

streets, inside shopping centers, and even partner opportunities at existing stores (shop shares). Last year, Appear Here was behind the launch of 4,000 pop-up shops in London alone, and it has worked with brands like Google, LVMH, Net-a-Porter, Topshop, Supreme, and Spotify. "Brands want more flexibility than ever before," Appear Here CEO Ross Bailey has said. "Stores used to be opened as a sign of growth and for shopper convenience, but that's now matched online. Physical retail is still needed, but to tell a story. That demands more unique approaches."

And this is just one marketplace. The opportunities are there for temporary retail to take flight—in everyday dealings with landlords, shopping center developers, or with builders of public, communal space. Sometimes a three-month pop-up becomes a six-year retail store, and sometimes it doesn't. Either way, it's becoming easier than ever to make a splash.

Nomadic Retail

In an age where declining store traffic is the order of the day, retailers and brands are finding new, inventive means of taking the brand to the people, versus waiting for the people to come to it. This concept of nomadic retailing—or "rogue retailing," as I like to call it, is changing the game for many brands.

Let's start with a case history on a sister market—the exploding world of the food truck. In 2008, just as the recession hit, hundreds of food truck vendors emerged on local foodie scenes, bringing unique, gourmet cuisine to the masses and changing the perception of what it meant to eat food-truck fare. What began in über-hip cities like Portland, Austin, and Los Angeles has become a worldwide phenomenon, where food-truck parks and walk-up dining are the norm in nearly every city. Food trucks generated about $2.7 billion in revenue in 2017, a fourfold increase from 2014 (according to the National Restaurant Association).

Now, and for the last five years or so, we are seeing the retail industry mobile up and take their show on the road. Simple pop-ups have transformed into fully nomadic retail trucks, buses, trailers, and even scooters, making brands as nimble as ever.

From start-ups and young e-commerce brands looking to establish a brick-and-mortar presence to legacy global brands attempting to test a new regional market or launch a new product or category, pop-up retail has become mainstream.

Always on the move, they drive up to any place where large groups of people might take interest (farmers' markets, music festivals, fashion events, etc.). These fully mobile and transformable environments are changing retail marketing as we know it.

A slew of "fashion trucks" have hit the road, getting products into the hands of the locals, if only for a day—or even an hour. Miami-based accessories brand Miansai can be seen trucking its leather goods and signet rings from any one of its fleet of five, including a 1965 Piaggio Scooter, a 1976 Fiat, or a 1949 Airstream trailer. "This mobile retail concept works because we're able to test markets without having to commit to formal leases or be locked into a specific place," says Miansai's founder and creative director Michael Saiger. "It gives us the opportunity to be agile and location-independent, which is really cool."

In a consumer world where flash mobs are a thing and social media can gain instant viral marketing effectiveness, pop-ups are fueling a whole new selfie-powered world.

Direct-to-consumer e-commerce brand True & Co., a line of women's lingerie, launched a mobile "try-on bar" where loyal customers can step into a transformed truck and get professionally fitted for a bra. In 2016, Canadian financial company Desjardins Group rolled out a pilot project called the Mobile Branch, a giant bank on wheels that could go wherever its customers needed it, during public events or even natural disasters. The Mobile Branch offered ATM services as well as a confidential space where customers could conduct transactions or speak with a Desjardins advisor. "Consumer behavior is always changing, and we've got to find solutions

to adapt," said Guy Cormier, president and CEO of Desjardins Group.

In-store Collaborations

Pop-ups are also a beneficial marketing tool for a retailer to test new and innovative product categories or partnerships in a temporary, low-risk setting. While enabling experimentation for the retailer, they also keep the in-store product mix fresh and differentiated, which drives more foot traffic. Nordstrom, for example, is taking advantage of these benefits. The retailer launched its constantly changing Pop-In@Nordstrom program in 2014, and it's still going strong into 2018. Launched as a shop-in-shop initiative, each temporary installation and product mix receives a four- to twelve-week run and is curated by Olivia Kim, Nordstrom's vice president of creative projects. A quick search of the hashtag #nordstrompop shows an exciting new spirit that Nordstrom has been able to inject into its stores. In a three-year run through both in-store shops and dedicated online websites and blogs, Nordstromites have had the luxury of buying from partner brands such as Liberty London, Warby Parker, Opening Ceremony, Aesop, Vans, Alexander Wang, Gentle Monster, goop, Hanes, and Everlane, with more continually coming.

In an interview with Fashionista.com in 2014, Kim said, "It's really important to me that not everything has to be a big production, it can feel very guerrilla and very true pop-up. I spend a lot of time with my buying team, looking for new things, collaborating with designers, coming up with special products just for us, and I work with my creative team to see what the website looks like, what are some cool functionalities that

Brands are activating their products in new ways, popping up where it makes the most sense.

we can do on the website: Can we do videos instead of flat product shots? Can we have a video game? How do we interact? How do we engage our customers? I spend a lot of time in meetings, that's kind of the worst part."

In looking at another side of the industry, shopping center developer General Growth Properties just launched a new "connected store" concept in Chicago, aimed at curating temporary themed products in a tech-driven shop. Located at Water Tower Place (a GGP property), the store is called IRL (In Real Life) and features digitally native brands based on a particular theme. The launch theme of "Home and Living" featured a combination of e-commerce brands from Leesa mattresses to Kassatex bathroom decor. The store stocks no inventory outside of the products on display, and all brands must be able to drop-ship to interested customers. Every few months, the theme changes, bringing a slew of new products with it. For GGP, it's a win-win, bringing fresh, up-and-coming digital brands into the physical space and changing everything out just often enough to attract foot traffic over and over again.

Brand Activation

New concepts to "bring the brand to life" are emerging, as consumers are looking for ways to better connect with the brands they love. In a recent survey, global insights agency Protein found that 79 percent of respondents expressed a desire for a closer relationship with retailers' physical communities. This is why we might find a Jack Daniel's activation at a country music festival, or a Harley Davidson gear truck at a motorcycle convention. Brands are activating their products in new ways, popping up where it makes the most sense.

Best Buy, Google, and Amazon have all been experimenting with pop-ups in the past few years, often in malls or temporary public spaces and typically when debuting a new product or service (i.e., Alexa or Google Home) for customers to engage with, test, try, and play with.

But technology is not the only sector of the market diving into the pop-up scene.

In June 2016, the Kellogg's NYC cereal café opened to a flood of media attention, inviting fans to reimagine the cereal experience. The brand was at a turning point, realizing that eating cereal for breakfast was losing steam with health-conscious Millennial consumers. So, what to do? Well, Kellogg's partnered with local culinary and hospitality experts Anthony Rudolf and Sandra Di Capua to elevate cereal combinations and create a menu that would surprise and delight the cereal enthusiast and New York tourist alike. On offer were interesting combos like Special K with Frosted Flakes, pistachios, lemon zest, and thyme, or Rice

Krispies paired with fresh strawberries and green tea powder. The store closed after a year, but the word on the street is that Kellogg's is looking for a bigger space in downtown Manhattan.

Brand activations are nothing new for Kellogg's. Back in 2010, the company experimented with its first-ever retail store and café—Pop-Tarts World in Times Square—which featured interactive displays, entertainment, and a whimsical store design and menu of more than 30 original Pop-Tarts creations. Interactive touchscreen stations featured Pop-Tarts games, a T-shirt

personalization station, and a "varietizer" that allowed guests to create custom-mixed boxes of Pop-Tarts to take home.

Speaking of customization, a pop-up experience that has resonated with me over the last years came from the least likely of candidates: Glade. Back in 2014, the candle and home fragrance brand opened an experiential pop-up in New York's Meatpacking District during the holiday season, touting itself as "the first store in the world to sell feelings." Intrigued, I had to check it out. Outside the space there was no Glade signage, no brand logo—only a neon-lit keyhole window display that read "WHAT WILL YOU FEEL?" Upon entering, visitors were asked to complete a brief profile on an iPad and to immerse themselves in the experience. In the back, a total of five rooms, each labeled with a word sign—ENERGY, ANTICIPATION, RELAX, FLIRTY, and FRESH AND NEW—offered varied multisensory experiences. In the ENERGY space, I was asked to sit in an audio-enhanced Egg Chair and put on a VR headset; the next thing I know, I was flying through clouds over mountaintops, a crisp, light scent radiating throughout. In the FLIRTY space, I took a picture in a gorgeous gown, holding a parasol, while scents of rose petals wafted by. In RELAX, I sat on a cloud of cotton, engrossed in the scent of fresh linens. It was a memorable, visceral, engaging experience—not to mention entertaining. And, best of all, free! Photos from my time in each room were emailed to me after the fact, along with a coupon for Glade fragrances, which I did, in fact, purchase and use when I returned home. And I still do to this day, because that brand jumped off the shelf at me the next time I was at my local Target, and continues to do so.

Whether you are selling candles, Pop-Tarts, lingerie, or banking services, pop-up retail has become a permanent part of the retail landscape. Temporary is the new permanent. As the saying goes, "All good things must come to an end." At least until the next good thing opens. <

ARCHITECTURE AT LARGE

Many decades have passed since Roland Barthes dubbed cars the cathedrals of modernity. Today, there is little doubt that our sacred places are the lavish retail environments on bustling high streets. Look no further than the designs of Rafael de Cárdenas and his prolific practice, Architecture at Large, to study some particularly awe-inspiring examples.

American-born designer Rafael de Cárdenas claims to be less interested in design than in human behavior, merging both aspects of architecture into interiors that draw us in. The New York City flagship store that he and his team recently designed for eyewear brand Gentle Monster envelops its entrants by virtue of striking visual effects. "The space could be the reincarnation of the giant, worm-like creature from *The Empire Strikes Back*, that nearly swallows the Millennium Falcon," explains de Cárdenas. "It's a figure that feels relevant to a lot of my work."

Cartier Pop-Up, Tokyo

By Rafael de Cárdenas

An extravagant Tokyo home designed by celebrated Japanese architect Tadao Ando provided the ideal environment for Rafael de Cárdenas's temporary space for Cartier, which draws upon the color black that is so often associated with Japanese design.

De Cárdenas's design does not attempt to mask the fact that this multifunctional space is housed within a domestic setting, instead using everyday furnishings—dining table, writing desk, and built-in shelving—to display Cartier's luxury wares.

The so-called Exogorth, or space slug, from the *Star Wars* movies is based on the biblical story of *Jonah and the Whale*, an archetypal account of journeying into the belly of the beast. Applied to retail, it may conjure up Debordian images of a consumer overpowered by commercial spectacle, and perhaps this picture is not entirely plucked out of the air. But as Leia, Chewbacca, and Jonah know, the beast can emerge as a blessing.

Besides relating back to famous reference points from "a galaxy far far away," de Cárdenas's work is inspired by worldly architectural structures designed "a long time ago." Take, for instance, the great gothic cathedrals, which he praises as the most skillfully laid out buildings in history. "The way they carry you, from narthex to nave to chapel, through anticipation, awe, and more contemplative states, >

De Cárdenas likes to employ reflections and color in order to structure and extrude space and create illusions and surreal atmospherics.

**Unknown Union,
Cape Town**

Architect Rafael de Cárdenas's scheme for a menswear store in Cape Town, South Africa, centers on a series of modular display units. Stacking cubes of varying heights and depths are painted in vibrant shades of blue, yellow, green, pink, and red—sometimes clashing and sometimes merging.

is just beyond compare. Maybe subconsciously I organize retail spaces along those lines: into zones of anticipation, crescendo, and ease."

Ease is not necessarily what comes to mind in the context of shopping, but de Cárdenas and Architecture at Large's (RDC/AAL) retail designs manage to soothe our senses. They do not achieve this by being minimal or timeless—not at all. Rather, they radiate a simultaneity of styles that thwarts the fast flow of trends and—much like the Exogorth creature—appear to exist beyond time. De Cárdenas likes to employ reflections and color in order to structure and extrude space, and create illusions and surreal atmospherics. As kaleidoscopic mirrored cabinets, his work produces moods and perspectives that both break and complement each other.

Having gained global recognition with their bold interiors for the art gallery OHWOW (now Moran Bondaroff) in Los Angeles and the menswear boutique Unknown Union in Cape Town, RDC/AAL has come to design classy stores for clients such as Nike and Cartier. Browsing the firm's extensive >

Rather than relying on one signature style, de Cárdenas and his team use cultural references to produce an atmosphere.

portfolio, which also includes residential, furniture, and brand development projects, one finds a versatile visual language impossible to nail down. Rather than relying on one signature style, de Cárdenas and his team use cultural references to produce an atmosphere: "Our process often begins with creating a fantasy around the brand we're working with. We analyze and mythologize the brand and its customers to create narratives about it. We do this in a few different ways and present the client with options. At that point, we usually end up turning down the volume, so to speak, on our initial ideas and, from there, start to work on a much finer level of detail."

De Cárdenas traces his eye for detail back to the time when he still worked on the intimate scale of garment construction: "Studying fashion attuned me to a certain finer grain of detail that I think often gets overlooked in the world of interior design," he says. Presumably, his first career also honed the designer's fine feel for multilayered, mixed-media compositions. "The choice of materials is always a polysensory consideration. Tactility, acoustic dynamics, and so forth, are all incredibly important considerations."　　>

Au Pont Rouge, St. Petersburg

The predominantly linear plan of de Cárdenas's scheme, which occupies an entire floor of the building, is punctuated by circular clearings that host a range of pop-up shops, events, and services, including a tattoo parlor and a barber shop.

Among the more notable elements in Rafael de Cárdenas's design for the store is his treatment of the ceilings. In one area, waves of textured anodized aluminum are punctuated with light fittings. Elsewhere, green fins alternate with neon tubing.

When working on retail environments that do attract crowds, like the 1,000-square-meter third floor of the department store Au Pont Rouge in St. Petersburg, de Cárdenas works to convey a feeling of exclusivity.

De Cárdenas's interest in spatial design was first sparked while working for Calvin Klein in the 1990s. He recalls how he was "particularly inspired by what Alexandre de Betak was doing at the time: his shows that were performances more than anything, and very much about affect." Dubbed the "Fellini of Fashion" for his runway pyrotechnics, de Betak famously broke the boundaries between fashion, art, and design. Fascinated with the producer's venturous, all-encompassing vision, de Cárdenas decided to widen his professional scope; he enrolled at UCLA and, as his first architectural project after graduation, designed a cathedral-like proposal for the redevelopment of the World Trade Center site with his mentor Greg Lynn. Following a stint at the brand strategy firm Imaginary Forces, he founded his own company in 2006.

Like de Betak's elaborate runway shows, many of RDC/AAL's retail environments are less designed to draw masses than to indulge a chosen few. Nike's Showroom in NYC's Soho district, which they designed in 2015, is conceived as an invitation-only fitness club. Shape Your Time, a temporal   >

environment for Cartier, was tucked away in a sub-urban Tokyo home and only opened to host exclusive dinners. When working on retail environments that do attract crowds, like the 1,000-square-meter third floor of the department store Au Pont Rouge in St. Petersburg, de Cárdenas works to convey a feeling of exclusivity. "Many retail experiences are not at all exclusive, considering the sheer number of people participating, but a well worked out store still gives customers the impression of being special. It's a delicate thing. What design cannot do has to be engineered through loyalty programs, memberships, and so forth."

Imbued with memories and cinematic moods from his 1980s youth, de Cárdenas's interiors evoke familiar images, but do so subtly—somewhat subconsciously even. Asked about the most palpable pop cultural influence on his work, the designer names

"The answer is never as simple as inserting technology; but beyond that, there is no one approach." The most important thing remains an authentic atmosphere.

Tony Scott's erotic vampire classic *The Hunger*, "specifically those scenes of Catherine Deneuve in diffuse light and shadow, playing the piano."

Speaking of references, Architecture at Large is perhaps, quite literally, architecture at liberty: In freeing the retail interior from being mere brand image, de Cárdenas allows it to become a "tissue of quotations," to once again borrow from Barthes. Particularly enjoyable embodiments of modern-day myth, RDC/AAL's interiors involve the viewer as a producer of space. "Not at all a passive, subdued retail experience," their Gentle Monster flagship creates an "elaborate effect of disorientation" through a carefully calibrated maze of one-way mirrors. Once swallowed by the space, one navigates through a diffuse narrative. "Mazes are a useful tool in retail," says de Cárdenas. "They make you feel lost—pleasantly, refreshingly so." <

Delfina Delettrez Boutique, London

For Delfina Delettrez's London boutique, Rafael de Cárdenas created an environment that reflects the jewelry designer's fascination with shape and texture. An unexpected mix of stainless steel and satin brass alongside fur and green faux-malachite leather is reflected to infinity in green-tinted mirrors.

CARTIER Precious Garage

On the occasion of Milan Design Week 2017, DESI SANTIAGO was commissioned to design a temporary venue names Precious Garage for luxury jeweler Cartier—a fantastical mix of gold, car parts, and jewelry, quite literally set within a car mechanic's workshop.

The four-day extravaganza was a vehicle for launching Cartier's Ecrou de Cartier line alongside pieces from the ever-popular Juste un Clou collection, first launched in the 1970s. At the heart of the spectacle, held in a genuine garage on Via delle Fosse Ardeatine, the bodywork of a 1978 Corvette C3 with Cartier license plates rises from the car mechanic's pit, with liquid gold spilling out over the floor instead of oil. Beside it, in a display case, the car's innards, also coated in gold, are displayed like pieces of art. On the workbench are plexiglass cases containing the jewelry. This installation is the work of New York visual artist and creative director Desi Santiago, who is known for his cerebral approach to set and costume designs. Here, his link with the workshop is not a casual one—anyone looking closely at the Cartier jewelry on display will see that its designs are inspired by nuts and bolts and masonry nails. <

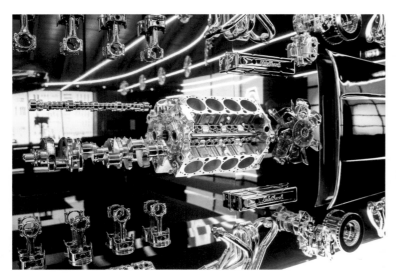

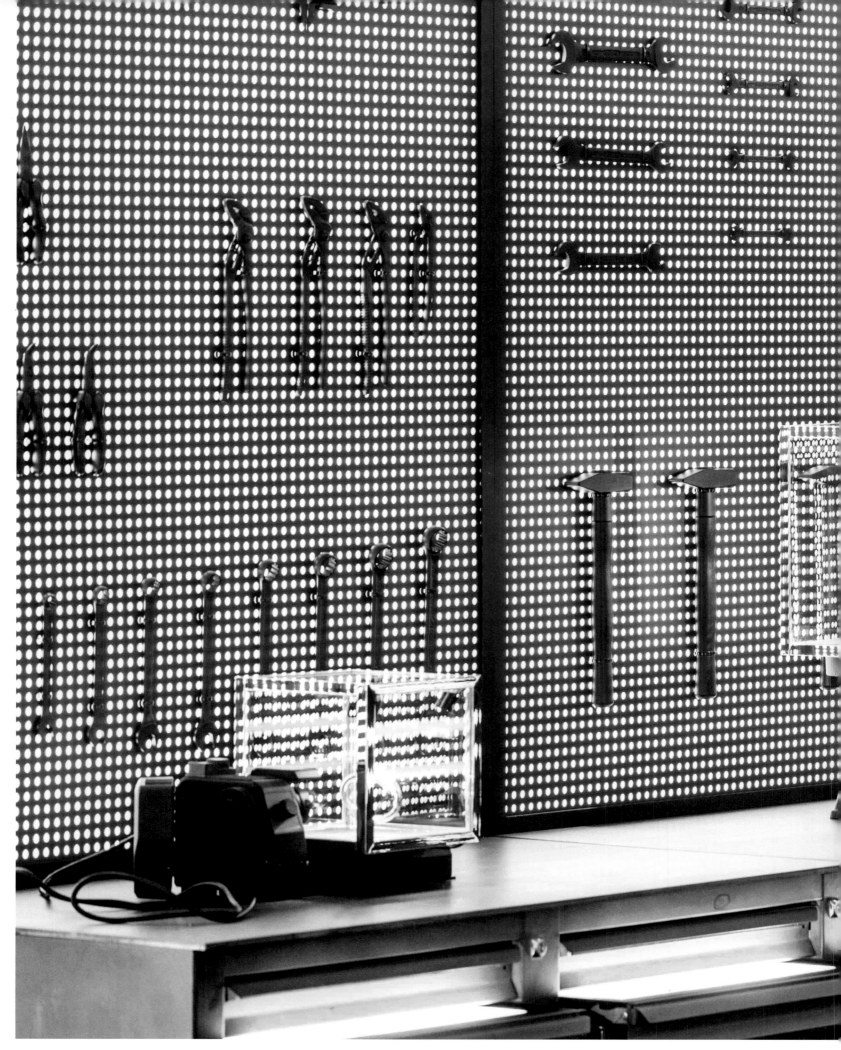

CADILLAC Experiential Space

When Cadillac moved its headquarters from Detroit to New York in 2015, the iconic automaker enlisted the services of global architectural firm GENSLER to help realize their vision of the future.

Step into Cadillac House in New York's SoHo neighborhood and you are immediately struck by the dynamism and state-of-the-art flair that design firm Gensler has injected into the brand's headquarters. Seeking to encapsulate the elegance for which the iconic American automobile manufacturer is renowned, Gensler has created what they call an experiential brand center. Serving as a rotating space for events and corporate collaborations, the massive showroom also houses a public café and lounge area, an exhibition space, and an outdoor terrace. But its true focus is the mirrored runway on which the latest Cadillac models are displayed in all their glory. To help develop a shifting marketing strategy for the brand, Gensler has equipped the space with highly integrated technology through which customers can fully experience the entire Cadillac portfolio. <

NOVELTY Boutique

In the exclusive suburb of San Pedro Garza García in the city of Monterrey, Mexico, ANAGRAMA has given shape to an intriguing interior design for women's clothing store Novelty, making it not only novel by name, but also by nature.

This high-end boutique caters to young women with a taste for fresh, modern fashion. The brand handpicks clothes and accessories that won't be found in other stores, but have the potential to set trends—hence the store's name, Novelty. In seeking the right look for such a store, Mexican design firm Anagrama wanted to emphasize the brand's idiosyncratic approach. Within a vast space set on two levels, the team created a wondrous world that is not unlike an Escher drawing. Filled with sets of stairs seemingly at odds with one another beneath a zigzag ceiling, the studio's design interferes with accepted conventions of perspective and form. Within this scene, Novelty's clothing is displayed minimally in glass cases or on finely figured marble plinths in colors that complement the interior design—jet black, pastel pink, and dove gray. The elements come together seamlessly, sharing sober yet feminine characteristics that awaken a curiosity in the brand's desired clientele. <

Accent lighting throughout the store gives structure to the bold geometric shapes that dominate its interior design, while smooth finishes such as polished plaster, metals, and marble reflect the femininity of the brand.

NOVELTY Boutique

MOLECURE PHARMACY Store

Taiwan outfit WATERFROM DESIGN redefines the concept of pharmacy for the third-generation owner of Molecure Pharmacy. Their scheme combines natural elements with a high-tech shop display to provide customers with an engaging experience.

In designing this showroom for the Molecure Pharmacy, whose name is a melding of the words "molecule" and "cure," Waterfrom Design created a series of display elements that aim, metaphorically, to represent various stages of the pharmaceutical process. At the heart of the retail space, dubbed "green in the lab," a block-wood laboratory table stands on a section of ancient tree trunk and contains a display of green plants. The ensemble reminds us that many pharmaceuticals originate from natural ingredients. Juxtaposed with this, and set against walls of white cobblestone, an almost transparent network of acrylic shelving lends a sanatory feel to the display of products. A copper spiral staircase that rises up through the store hints at the structure of DNA, creating that all-important link to our well-being. This refreshing, innovative approach removes the stuffy atmosphere of the pharmacies we are more familiar with. The scheme achieves a perfect balance between the clinical nature of the pharmaceutical business and a more engaging, ultimately personal, experience for the customer. <

EXPERIENTIAL RETAIL

KATHARINA MICHALSKI—Trend Researcher, Founder of Culture Dots

In an increasingly competitive and challenging retail landscape, brick-and-mortar stores must establish unique identities to stay relevant. With a focus on brand experience rather than sales, retailers have become more proactive in how they increase foot traffic and enhance engagement.

According to a recent survey by Influenster, while Black Friday is the busiest shopping day in the United States, only one in three millennials plans to buy in-store. In 2015, the figure was almost twice as high. Meanwhile, 62 percent intend to use their mobile devices for Black Friday shopping. Rather than suggesting the imminent demise of physical retail, these figures confirm what has been looming for a while: online and offline commerce are no longer the same. As they start playing to their respective strengths, two unique forms of shopping emerge.

Online shopping offers convenience and efficiency. It is well-suited to bargain-hunting consumers seeking to avoid the hassle and inconvenience of being in an overcrowded, busy store. Instead, what they have come to expect from brick-and-mortar is a sense of discovery and connection. Retailers competing with e-commerce on stock and price are bound to struggle. Those who thrive in the current retail landscape do not see brick-and-mortar in opposition to e-commerce; they view it as its enhancement.

More and more, brands are rediscovering physical retail as a marketing channel. For example, home sound system manufacturer Sonos sees its first U. K. store as a place to discover the brand and get excited about their products. Its success won't be measured by direct sales, but rather on how many people visit the store and leave with a concrete intention to buy or recommend the brand. Of course, Sonos hopes to increase sales, but is agnostic about where customers buy product. Brands like Sonos recognize that the real world offers the opportunity to connect with customers on a

deeper level. At the same time, customers increasingly expect retail stores to be an extension of how they view the world. In response to this changing climate, brick-and-mortar has become more experiential.

The main premise of experiential retail is customer-centricity. Whether fulfilling a need they didn't know they had, solving a problem at the brand's expense, or simply making the shopping experience as compelling and seamless as possible, customer experience matters more than ever. With this goal in mind, retailers pay closer attention to store atmosphere and design, and look outside their respective category for inspiration. In addition to designing exciting in-store environments that can resemble hotel lobbies, retailers invest time and money in selecting, training, and empowering their staff.

For example, sportswear brand Outdoor Voices seeks staff that are into sports and able to organize community

The challenge for retailers goes beyond being more memorable than everyday shopping; it is about utilizing the three-dimensional space to truly connect with customers through enriching experiences.

events in their local areas. Aesop's store managers are expected to build relationships with cool local businesses such as hotels, cafés, and restaurants. Pret A Manger allows its staff to give away free drinks to regular visitors, customers who spend a lot,

and those with whom they have a nice conversation. Being experiential means turning store employees into brand ambassadors who are instrumental in building relationships with customers.

The biggest challenge to this relationship is when problems and failures occur. In such situations, the staff's interpersonal skills are put to the test as their communication during the recovery decides the outcome. Since every situation is different, their response cannot be scripted.

Retailers competing with e-commerce on stock and price are bound to struggle. Those who thrive in the current retail landscape do not see brick-and-mortar in opposition to e-commerce; they view it as its enhancement.

Paradoxically, this opens a window of opportunity for the brand to not only restore trust but also exceed customers' expectations. Ogilvy's executive creative director Rory Sutherland also recognizes the potential in failure recovery. "If a customer has a problem and a brand resolves it in a satisfactory manner, the customer becomes a more loyal customer than if the fault had not occurred in the first place," Sutherland wrote in a piece for The Marketing Society. Osman Khan, founder and director at the Institute of Customer Management, found that a well-managed recovery can create a memorable experience because it forces the brand to respond to the customer in a unique manner. Echoing Sutherland, he notes that the more memorable experience the customer has with the brand, the more emotionally attached they become. On the other hand, a bad service recovery creates a negative emotional response that lasts longer if the retailer doesn't intervene. Empowering staff to act quickly in the best

interest of the customer can make all the difference between a loyal customer and a lapsed one.

Sephora is a good example of a retailer that truly understands that a relationship built on trust can benefit the brand. The beauty chain is currently experimenting with a concept called Sephora Studio, which is a pared-down version of their flagship stores that focuses on fostering a personal connection between clients and beauty advisors.

The smaller space requires the retailer to be much more selective when it comes to their brand and product selection, and offering choice is not the priority. Instead, the in-store experience revolves around eight makeup stations where customers can receive personal consultations and tap into the expertise of Sephora's beauty advisors. During a consultation, the advisor can take pictures of the client, note all the

Whether fulfilling a need they didn't know they had, solving a problem at the brand's expense, or simply making the shopping experience as compelling as possible, customer experience matters more than ever.

products they tested, and then email the list to them or add it to their online profile. Technology is used to assist relationship building. Taking cues from the likes of Apple, Sephora has eliminated cash registers and equipped staff with iPhones to process payments digitally.

The most immediate goal of experiential retail is to increase foot traffic. Sephora Studio not only removes barriers to purchase but also creates reasons to visit the store. Like Sephora Studio, many other retailers have started adding experiential elements to their stores to draw in customers. Food, for example, has become a major experiential driver. Shopping malls are much more selective in choosing restaurants and cafés that offer shoppers the best mix of retail and food. Retailers team up with hospitality partners to offer an aspirational lifestyle that consumers want to be part of.

Creating memorable experiences relies on techniques for attracting and holding attention. The more participatory the experience, the more captivated and engaged the customer will be.

Luxury department store Harrods is currently upgrading its historic Food Hall to include experiential elements like a bakery and coffee roaster.

However, attaching a food outlet to a store does not always makes sense, so retailers are exploring different ways to offer customers unique in-store experiences. For instance, Nike launched Makers' Experience at Nike By You Studio @ 45 Grand in New York, an invite-only design experience that allows customers to leave with personalized sneakers in less than 90 minutes. By comparison, Nike's online customization tool takes six to eight weeks. Similarly, Vans offers customization at events and in stores. This is a natural extension of the brand's long-running Customs program, which launched with the opening of their first store in Anaheim in 1966. Back then, customers could bring their own fabric into the store and pay an extra charge for custom shoes. Today, an innovative machine prints any pattern, photo, or design onto a pair of shoes in less than 15 minutes. Vans views personalization as a way to connect with customers and give them a platform to express their creativity.

In a representative survey of 500 German consumers, KPMG found that more than half of the respondents were interested in personalized products, and only one in three had bought one; 58 percent of those who had already purchased customized products were under the age of 40. The heightened interest in customization is not surprising given how much value Western society places on individuality. In his latest book, *Wired* magazine founder Kevin Kelly anticipates an increase in personalized products and services because they tap into a fundamental need, as according to him, they "help to distill ourselves to a unique point [and] to optimize our personality."

In-store personalization not only addresses this need for distinction but also the desire for instant gratification; the ultimate strength of brick-and-mortar. And with the introduction of 3-D knitting

machines, it could become even bigger. Ministry of Supply, which makes bespoke performance clothes for the office, has permanently installed a 3-D knitting machine in their Boston flagship store that makes customizable jackets. Shoppers can choose the color of the body, the cuffs, and the buttons. It takes about 90 minutes to knit. The jacket then gets washed and dried so it's pre-shrunk. The price is only slightly above that of non-custom jackets and the brand plans to increase the customizable options to include fit.

Kelly believes that the value of experiences will increase because they remain the only scarcity in what he calls a "superabundant" society. Unlike material and digital things, experiences are truly unique and cannot be copied. Because humans excel at creating and consuming experiences, Kelly explains, "we will use technology to produce commodities, and we will make experiences in order to avoid becoming commodities ourselves." The mass-scale introduction of new technology during the Industrial Revolution not only created the need to escape the hustle and bustle of the city but also played a role in the rise of Romanticism, which emphasized emotion and individualism. In his best-selling book *Sapiens*, Yuval Noah Harari draws a parallel between today's experience economy and the Romanticism of the nineteenth century, which tells us that in order to make the most of our human potential we must have

The value of experiences will increase because they remain the only scarcity in what Kelly calls a "superabundant" society.

as many different experiences as we can. "Romanticism, which encourages variety, meshes perfectly with consumerism.

Their marriage has given birth to the infinite 'market of experiences,' on which the modern tourism industry is founded," writes Harari. However, our infatuation with experiences is not just the product of cultural change. Researchers have found that experiences are strongly linked to our identity, social connection, and happiness. While we sometimes regard possessions as extensions of ourselves, they nonetheless remain separate from us; but our memories and experiences really are part of who we are. As psychologist Thomas Gilovich put it, "We are the sum of our experiences." Experiences can reinforce social connection, as we tend to do things with or around other people. Because social interaction is one of the most important determinants of human happiness, making a spontaneous personal connection can positively influence how we feel. Although in the past our idea of happiness revolved around accumulating and owning things, materialism is now in decline. We now know that happiness associated with material things is fleeting. Although we can keep physical objects for a long time, they don't keep us happy for as long as a finite experience.

The once-desired material things quickly become part of the new normal, while even a mediocre experience can become a great story with time. In contrast to objects like cars and clothes, individual experiences are hard to compare and do not often cause status anxiety. What's more, the anticipation of an experience starts before you buy it. Psychologists even go as far as to say, if you can't live in the moment, it's best to live in anticipation of an experience. Consequently, making stores more experiential is an investment that can leave a lasting impression on its customer.

It is crucial for brands to understand what their consumers want and to apply that knowledge in unique ways. Urban Outfitters, for example, recognized that millennial shoppers seek unique experiences

Happiness associated with material things is fleeting. Although we can keep physical objects for a long time, they don't keep us happy for as long as a finite experience.

that reflect their individuality. With that in mind, the clothing company opened three concept retail shops: Space 15 Twenty in Los Angeles, California, Space Ninety 8 in Williamsburg, New York, and Space 24 Twenty in Austin, Texas. Described as "gathering places curated specifically for the local community," each store combines retail, dining, events, pop-ups, and artist collaborations.

The New York location spans five floors and houses retailers, galleries, and a rooftop restaurant and bar. Among a recent event line-up, a plant workshop taught participants how to pot plants and make

plant-shaped ice cream, all while enjoying live music and kombucha. Other happenings included an edible art installation with sensorial drinks and music performances, and a discussion on how tarot cards and magic can benefit entrepreneurship and creative thinking.

The Los Angeles store recently hosted a preview of the Juicy Couture for UO collaboration with a 2000s-inspired launch party that included a free performance by Tinashe. Personalization was offered with any Juicy Couture purchase as guests were able to get custom embroidery by chain stitch masters Lot, Stock and Barrel. Creating memorable experiences relies

Food has become a major experiential driver. Retailers team up with hospitality partners to offer an aspirational lifestyle that consumers want to be part of.

on techniques for attracting and holding attention. The more participatory the experience, the more captivated and engaged the customer will be. Workshops in which participants learn a manual or creative skill are an example of active participation. Being engaged in a skilled practice means attending to the experience in a sustained way instead of simply watching it. On the other end of the spectrum, passive experiences are best exemplified by our cultural obsession with visual media and the selfie. Driven by the sudden rise of Instagram, the photograph has become the experience itself. The demand for trendy environments as photo-worthy backdrops is changing how people approach travel destinations, increasingly giving preference to visiting the most Instagrammed locations over historic and cultural sights. The Museum of Ice Cream became an Instagram sensation by offering the perfect setting for a highly sharable image, like a pool filled with sprinkles that visitors can dive into. Although not as extreme, nearly all retailers, hotels, and restaurants are also paying more attention to how Instagram-ready their spaces are.

While a beautiful backdrop can create Instagram fame for a retailer, it is short-lived. On the other hand, an outstanding customer experience can leave a lasting impression. The challenge for retailers goes beyond being more memorable than everyday shopping; it is about utilizing the three-dimensional space to truly connect with customers through enriching experiences. Experiences are only valuable if they tune into the needs of the customer, be it personal attention, individual distinction, or social connection. This investment in a relationship between a retailer and the customer can create a lasting bond, which ultimately translates to sales. <

PATOM Shop & Showroom

NITAPROW's eco-conscious showroom, store, and café for Patom Organic Living's body care products oozes "nature" inside and out. Taking cues from the local environment, the design is high-tech and modern with a distinctly sustainable, organic vibe.

When commissioned to design a store for Patom Organic Living, architects Nitaprow had the luxury of starting from scratch. The brief was to design a store that could function as both a showroom and café for Patom's organic body care products as well as a center for raising ecological awareness and sustainable living through a series of workshops and farmers' markets. Though the design they created in the lush setting is unabashedly high-tech and modern, Nitaprow's concept is truly organic in every respect. Inspired by the radiating branches of the coconut and palm trees at Patom's organic farm, the building's elegant, double-height frame is made from reclaimed wood. Floor-to-ceiling glass walls allow for verdant garden views, while people are drawn in by an equally natural-looking environment for Patom's products, displayed on tables made from fallen trees that sit on warm, raw concrete screed. Inside, there are just enough curves to facilitate both the physical and visual flow and reconnect the interior design language with that of the landscape outside. <

Bliss Foundation circa ... universities, governments ... and the private sector to ... agriculture in Nakhon Pathom and the neighbouring provinces under the 'Sampran Model'.

The movement started a while ago at Sampran Riverside together with funding support from Thailand Research Fund (srf) and Thai Health Promotion Foundation (ssss).

At present, there are over 130 families of organic farmers divided into 11 groups producing rice, vegetables and fruits under Sookjai Organics POS (Participatory Guarantee System).

To learn more, please visit
www.sampranmodel.com

The rattan-wrapped spiral staircase with circular mezzanine is the focal point of the room. Not only does it offer a privileged view of the store, but its curvaceous form serves to create flow in the predominantly rectilinear space.

THE KRUG ROOM Showroom & Restaurant

Hong Kong's Mandarin Oriental hotel celebrates its 50th anniversary by giving The Krug Room, its most exclusive dining salon, a stunning makeover. Zoning in on heritage and luxury, MAXIME DAUTRESME's creation is at once exuberant and charming.

Nestled in the heart of Mandarin Oriental's kitchen, and boasting one of the world's finest culinary experiences, The Krug Room was established in 2006 in a partnership with House of Krug champagne. When considering its refurbishment, Maxime Dautresme from the design studio Substance honed in on the exclusivity and intimacy of the room, which seats just 12 people. Their concept was to combine the utmost luxury of top-end dining with the good cheer that comes with drinking champagne. A handcrafted chandelier, fashioned from hammered brass and inspired by champagne nestled in ice, is suspended above a central, solid-marble table that is flanked on either side by shuttered windows. The effect is akin to sitting in the dining carriage of a train: raise the shutters, and you'll catch glimpses of the fast-moving kitchen beyond. A vaulted ceiling and walls covered in herringbone fabric contribute to the warm ambience of the room. The aesthetic encapsulates the feeling of heritage and craftsmanship represented by both the hotel and Krug champagne. <

BAR LUCE Café

In one of several collaborations with the luxury fashion brand, Prada, WES ANDERSON seeks to recreate the atmosphere of Milanese cafés in this one-off dining hall—a concept that lends itself perfectly to Anderson's somewhat surreal sense of style.

Spacious and gracious, Bar Luce is the main dining space within the Fondazione Prada, Milan—an arts center created by the fashion brand and housed in a converted distillery. Anderson pays homage to landmark cafés dotted around the city, many of which have changed little since 1950s and 1960s. As such, he makes abundant use of veneered wooden paneling and upholstered Formica furniture. The predominantly pastel palette is exemplified in the tutti-frutti terrazzo flooring—pink with flashes of red, gray, and white. Something of a rarity in today's climate of industrial, minimalist design, Anderson has used wallpaper with classical designs to accentuate the building's original features—most notably the gently undulating vaulted ceiling. Suspended above the room, two regimented rows of opal-glass pendant globes bathe diners in a warm, glowing light. Finishing touches include a jukebox, a pair of pinball machines featuring characters from Anderson's movies, and a teal-colored wall-mounted clock. <

BAR LUCE Café, Fondazione Prada, Milan

MAX&CO. Window Display

In STUDIOPEPE's surreal Minimal Terrarium shop-window display for MAX&Co.'s flagship store in Milan, a group of faceless mannequins wore identical outfits in different colors as they admired oversized foliage.

Design agency Studiopepe has collaborated with the Max Mara Fashion Group since 2012 to produce interiors and window displays for the brand's MAX&Co. division. Aimed at a younger customer, MAX&Co. utilizes innovative materials and contemporary designs to create a complete wardrobe for the modern woman. Known for a somewhat eclectic style that builds on unusual associations to create not just a visual impact but also an emotional one, Studiopepe is a perfect match for the brand. Rather than attempt to show the brand's entire collection in one display, Studiopepe focused on a single element: that season's mohair coat and matching baseball cap. The mannequins were arranged in lifelike poses in a setting that hinted loosely at a botanical garden with oversized plants and wire cages. The mannequins appeared frozen in time during a shared conversation or experience, or while simply taking in the scene. The surreal minimalism is common to all of Studiopepe's window displays for the brand, which have featured special occasion dresses in a woodland setting and chic everyday wear in a chocolate factory. <

T FONDACO DEI TEDESCHI Window Display

In a series of exquisite floral displays commissioned by the Venetian T Fondaco dei Tedeschi department store, Swedish designer JOANN TAN creates her own interpretation of the magical city and evokes memories of the merchant traders of yesteryear.

Joann Tan's creations are so wondrous that you could easily forget that they are shop displays. Whether she is commissioned to promote jewelry, fragrance or footwear, the merchandise becomes so integral to her design that you may fail to spot it at first glance. This was certainly the case for a range of blooms that Joann Tan Studio created for the prestigious T Fondaco dei Tedeschi in Venice, Italy. Originally the site of a merchant trading hall, T Fondaco dei Tedeschi opened as a department store in 2017, following an extensive and expensive refurbishment. Housing four floors of luxury brands, its opening was highly anticipated. For her window blooms, Tan focused on the environment surrounding the store's location. Inspired by the little pockets of green you stumble upon when walking the streets of Venice, she created a series of plants she envisaged growing there. Modeling her designs on eighteenth-century botanical illustrations makes them strangely evocative of merchant travels. <

ONDACO DEI TEDESCHI DFS

T FONDACO DEI TEDESCHI Window Display

There is pure exoticism in the way Joann Tan grafts merchandise onto her works of flora and fauna. So magical are her creations that they resemble treasures collected by Venetian merchants on their travels in faraway lands.

BERGDORF GOODMAN Window Display

A collaboration between British designer LEE BROOM and New York's prestigious Bergdorf Goodman department store culminated in a series of illuminated window displays that presented the latest menswear in a whole new light.

Known for his innovative lighting design, Lee Broom used light as the focus of his playful window displays for the landmark New York retailer, located at the crossroads of fashion at 5th Avenue and 58th Street. Established in 1901, Bergdorf Goodman showcases leading and emerging designers, and epitomizes fine style and modern luxury. So what better partner for the department store than an award-winning British light designer whose pieces, made of Carrara marble, crystal, and polished brass, complement the exquisite fabrics of the finely crafted clothing on display? Commissioned by Shane Ruth, Bergdorf's visionary visual director, Broom created four window displays examining the everyday life of a man through the themes Exercise, Work, Play, and Explore. Each presented a surreal landscape in which his lighting set the scene for the stylish outfits. Crystal bulbs were suspended like gems in a diamond mine and crescent lights resembled stellar objects in the night sky. <

BERGDORF GOODMAN Window Display

FENDI

Embedded in the luxury house's DNA, Fendi's unique approach to design is the driver upon which Silvia Venturini Fendi relies to foster independent creativity across all aspects of the brand. In partnering with Design Miami as its incubator and stage for design performances, Fendi brought to light a new generation of bright minds whose bold approach sets new standards in brand architecture.

"The universe of design is a never-ending passion and a source of continuous inspiration. It is a fascinating world, made of individuals with extraordinary personalities and invigorating, personal styles that shun the conventional. It provides a stimulus to dare, to experiment, to free our creativity and push ourselves beyond established limits," says Silvia Venturini Fendi, Fendi's Creative Director of Accessories, Menswear and Kidswear. It is a statement that has underlined the brand's dynamic retail and design strategy for the past decade.

Fendi has always been a step ahead when it comes to supporting design: in 2009, the fashion house initiated the Craft Punk movement in >

The Happy Room at Design Miami 2016

By Cristina Celestino

Fendi collaborated with architect and designer Cristina Celestino to create *The Happy Room,* a traveling VIP lounge for prestigious clients that first was introduced at Design Miami. References to the brand's signature style are synthesized in a collection of 12 custom-made design objects, and range from fox fur cast in plexiglass to compose unique screens and armchairs to table bases that resemble brass earring clasps.

THE HAPPY ROOM
FENDI and Cristina Celestino

FENDI presents THE HAPPY ROOM, a collection by the Italian designer Cristina Celestino who has conceived a refined selection of furnishings dedicated to the first traveling FENDI VIP Room. Celestino melds the traditional excellence of the Roman Maison with her fresh and enchanting approach. Envisioned as an intimate, private and personal experience closely linked to femininity and sophisticated elegance with a touch of irony, the project is designed to host FENDI clients worldwide.

With soft and rarefied tones distinguished by simple dimensions and rounded shapes, THE HAPPY ROOM implies harmony and privacy.

The references to FENDI's iconic elements are numerous, such as the distinctive repetition of the arch characterizing the Palazzo della Civiltà Italiana in Rome, inlaid materials, the contrasting play of various types of marbles and innovative techniques such as Etere, an experiment of fur within resin.
THE HAPPY ROOM introduces an inspired version of a modular VIP room.
It emphasizes and confirms once again FENDI's commitment to the world of design and the values that distinguish that world: creativity associated with excellence, quality of precise workmanship, mastery of execu[...] the Italian savoir faire.

FENDI

The house of FENDI was established by Adele and Edoardo Fendi in Rome in 1925.
The opening of the first FENDI boutique– a handbag shop and fur workshop followed.
Soon winning international acclaim, FENDI emerged as a brand renowned for its elegance, craftsmanship, innovatio[...] 1965, the collaboration [...] begins and continu[...]
In 199[...] seconds Karl L[...]tion. In 1994 she is [...]ther goods accessories [...]ion of the kidswear and [...]es.
In 2000 the LVMH Group acquires FENDI becoming in 2001 its majority shareholder. Since 2008 FENDI is partner with Design Miami/. Today FENDI is synonymous with quality, tradition, experimentation and creativity.

CRIST[...]

Cristina C[...] who has b[...] 2010. She[...] of Archite[...] to found [...] experime[...] After part[...] her desig[...] in Italy an[...] the perman[...] Triennale [...] In 2016, C[...] the 1 st E[...] Award "fo[...] between [...] ones, to [...] and for h[...] like frag[...] expressine[...] with the h[...]

86

...ed architect
...n field since
... the School
...nd went on
... where she
...n.
...ellite in 2012,
...alleries both
...come part of
...Design at the

...Jury Prize of
...obile Milano
...cting figure
...re seasoned
...erimentation,
...hing themes
...elicacy and
...ns fashioned
...ie industry."

The integration of design and craftsman-ship went from a creative venture to becoming a main pillar of Fendi's design ethos.

collaboration with Design Miami. As part of the design performance program, talents Simon Hasan, Yuri Suzuki+Household, Studio Libertiny, and Peter Marigold were invited to let their imaginations flow, working their low-tech magic with the help of discarded materials from Fendi's production process, including leather, FF-logo-branded fabrics, plastic decorative elements, and metal hardware. Fendi artisans were also available during the event to teach designers how to work with leather. The result was bold: garden hoses were turned into chairs, and discarded scraps of leather from Fendi's factories became tabletops.

That same year, the Italian luxury house launched an ongoing program of collaborations with designers: first, to emphasize approaches to production that blend the traditional and the experimental; second, to celebrate the creative process that plays a key role in adding value to the final products. "In 2012 Fendi invited us to develop Craftica, a new body of work exploring leather craft in conversation with other hand-worked, natural materials," design studio Studio Formafantasma recalls. "Craftica was more than a simple design project: it was a visual and tactile investigation into leather."

The integration of design and craftsmanship went from creative venture to a pillar of Fendi's design ethos. Designer projects began to inform the brand's approach to aesthetics, interiors, and the retail space.

Fendi as Design Incubator

"We started 10 years ago," Silvia Venturini Fendi explains. "Just as Design Miami as a fair and Miami as a city have grown, our interests and ties to the design world have also evolved. We have all witnessed tremendous changes, where creativity has fueled new forms of urbanity and defined new lifestyles.   >

FENDI Omotesando Pop-Up Store, Tokyo

By Cristina Celestino

Arranged on two floors, this playful pop-up store in Omotesando, Tokyo, encapsulates the luxury and craftsmanship of the brand, with an emphasis on its classical Italian origins. At basement level, The Happy Room makes its debut, the organic forms and soft harmonious tones of the furniture evoking a 1950s Italian vibe.

Palazzo Privé at Palazzo Fendi, Rome

By Dimore Studio

For the second floor of Palazzo Fendi the brand approached Dimore Studio, a Milan-based duo of designers, to create the so called *Palazzo Privé*: the opulently decorated Roman apartment creates an intimate atmosphere and is meant to host exclusive guests.

Ranging from performance and installation to interior design, this rich history of unusual collaborative projects points to how the luxury Italian brand nurtures its ties with the design community and unearths some of its boldest creative talents.

Miami has transformed thanks to design and art; objects now inform the Miami style," adds the Fendi visionary. A solid ground for creative exploration, Design Miami serves as a design incubator for the luxury fashion house: once commissioned and unveiled in their boldest form, projects can now be adapted, turned into creative assets within Fendi's retail empire. In return, Fendi acts as a patron, a springboard for talented minds. For example, when Fendi collaborated with Johanna Grawunder to design the façade of the Miami Design District boutique in 2015, it was with a clear visual design brief in mind. The luxury house had collaborated with Grawunder back in 2013, when she created striking light installations for the Fendi exhibition at Tokyo's Art University Museum. "We wanted the store concept to reflect the culture of its location—the colors, >

Inside the Palazzo's now edgy interiors, custom-made pieces by Dimore include a sculptural brass and glass tube installation and a monumental Pergamena leather and brass chandelier hanging over the dining room table.

the energy, the influence of design in the area," Pietro Beccari, Fendi's Chairman and CEO recalls. "We liked the idea of working with a creative mind for the façade, and Grawunder was a natural fit. Her use of light and color worked very well with the overall design concept we had in mind. Plus, her vibrant palette pays homage to the Miami culture."

Design Miami 2016 served as a stage for Cristina Celestino's The Happy Room, a VIP area where the Italian designer composed an interior using fur. "Fur is in Fendi's DNA. It is incredible how Cristina managed to approach it and transfigure it. Fur is soft; she gave it strength and projected into the future by solidifying it! One still feels the softness through the resin; petrified, the fur shines through with elegance. Cristina exalted it," Silvia Venturini Fendi concedes. For the brand, Celestino created a new special fur treatment under resin called Etere. This is seen in fur panels in which the alternating and contrasting materials give the fur an almost frosted, 3-D impression. "The frosting of fur is almost a way to make it eternal, yet it adds a touch of lightness," Celestino says. A definite twist on design, it was further staged in the brand's pop-up store in Tokyo in 2017.

Ranging from performance and installation to interior design, this rich history of unusual collaborative projects points to how the Italian luxury brand nurtures its ties with the design community and unearths some of its boldest creative talents.

Today design informs Fendi's visual language at a global level. From the façade to the walls, the interior design, and the products on display, design is embedded in every layer of Fendi's flagships, pop-up events, and retail spaces. "The vertical design concept that is unveiled in new stores," Beccari adds, "allows for a 'journey of emotion' with contrasting materials and a greater range of products to be showcased. Dualism is part of the Fendi DNA, and our stores often have a balance between light and dark materials, statutory elements, and visionary designs."

All Roads Lead to Rome

"Render unto Rome the things that are Rome's. Fendi is Rome, and Rome is Fendi. Fendi has a deep bond with Rome [so] funding key restoration projects was very important, not just as an act of philanthropy, but as a way to thank the eternal city for all that we have been given in these years," says Beccari. >

The dining room in Fendi's *Palazzo Privé* has walls washed in sage green and a bookcase made from lacquered metal and stained glass. Alongside custom pieces designed by Dimore Studio's Emiliano Salci and Britt Moran, vintage pieces such as Bruno Mathsson's *Miranda* lounge chair strike an elegant chord.

Palazzo Fendi, Rome

By Gwenael Nicolas

Marble floors, plush carpets, and "fur wall art" are signature themes at Fendi's flagship store in Rome, Palazzo Fendi, which houses not only the boutique designed by star architect Gwenael Nicolas (founder of Curiosity) but also a boutique hotel, ZUMA restaurant and rooftop bar. The brand's collections are arranged on two floors, united by a monumental staircase hewn from Lepanto marble. Dotted around the place are collectible design pieces both historic and contemporary ranging from Gio Ponti to the Campana brothers.

FENDI Palazzo Fendi, Rome

"We wanted the store concept to reflect the culture of its location—the colors, the energy, the influence of design in the area." —Pietro Beccari, Fendi Chairman and CEO

In homage to its home city, the brand has recently funded the restoration of monuments like the Quattro Fontane complex, the Trevi Fountain, and most notably the Palazzo della Civiltà Italiana, an icon of twentieth-century Roman architecture that now houses Fendi's headquarters. Therefore, in every store concept, Rome is never far away. Each store, for example, incorporates travertine and bronze—materials meant to recall the colors of Rome and its majestic skyline.

If the framework includes a vibrant homage to Rome's history, it is only the first layer; Fendi gives every designer a creative carte blanche, expecting a unique visual outcome for each of its stores. In 2014, Beccari, together with Venturini Fendi, commissioned the duo behind Dimore Studio to create a collection of design pieces for Design Miami in the lead-up to the Palazzo's refurbishment. Entitled "Roman Lounge," the well-received display featured two light sculptures, a black iron and smoked glass bookcase, a square dining table, two crocodile and leather armchairs, and a sheared mink–covered chaise longue, all of which were originally conceived for Fendi's apartment in Rome, also known as Salon privé. Designed by Emiliano Salci and Britt Moran of Dimore Studio, the apartment unfolds on the second floor of Palazzo Fendi, a seventeenth-century landmark building, >

Foglie di Pietra and *Abete* Sculptures

By Giuseppe Penone

Previous page_Foglie di Pietra (Leaves of Stone, 2016). Created by Giuseppe Penone, the steel and bronze tree sculpture was installed in front of Palazzo Fendi.

*Above_*Penone also installed a naked bronze tree sculpture named *Abete* in front of Palazzo della Civiltà Italiana, which houses Fendi's headquarters and where the sculpture remained from January 2017 to January 2018, aiming to establish a dialogue between the ancient city's past and its present.

FENDI Miami Design District Store Façade

By Johanna Grawunder

*Right_*Fendi's eye-catching Miami flagship is located in the city's Design District. The work of light-artist and designer Johanna Grawunder, the façade captures Miami's art deco heritage with a color-blocked design in deep orange and icy blue. Inside, bare-brick walls and cement floors present a deliberate contrast to the opulence of the brand's wares.

previously a characterless Fendi store and anony-
mous office space. The five-story gem was ambi-
tiously remolded and up-fitted as a cultural, retail,
hospitality, and entertaining complex for the brand
and its clients. "Seeing the pieces [commissioned for
Design Miami] in their ultimate destination is very
exciting," says Venturini Fendi. Inside the Palazzo's
now edgy interiors, custom-made pieces by Dimore
include a sculptural brass and glass tube installation
in the foyer, a wall sconce in the living room crafted from Fendi Selleria leather, and a monumental
Pergamena leather and brass chandelier hanging
over the dining room table.

Down a few floors, Palazzo Fendi isn't a simple
flagship boutique: the retail space combines the
Maison's commitment to creativity in all forms, from
its collections to its architecture to its ever-changing
installations created in collaboration with artists. The
latest art installation commissioned by Fendi was a
gift to the city of Rome: on Largo Goldoni, directly
across from Palazzo Fendi, famous Italian artist
Giuseppe Penone installed a permanent site-specific
sculpture. Entitled *Foglie di Pietra*, it features intertwined trees cast out of bronze and marble.

On the brand's design approach, Silvia
Venturini Fendi concludes: "The risk is always to be
too branded; to avoid that, design projects at Fendi
tend to have a life of their own. They have thrived
on freedom of expression for the past 10 years. We
all embarked on a collaborative journey. We never
had a marketing strategy: the process is organic.
Designers explore and experiment with the themes
and field they choose." <

"The risk is always to be too branded; to avoid
that, design projects at Fendi tend to have a life
of their own. They have thrived on freedom of expression for the past 10 years. We all embarked on
a collaborative journey."—Silvia Venturini Fendi

FENDI Ginza
Pop-Up Store, Tokyo

By Azuma Makoto

To celebrate the release of its flo-ral Spring/Summer 2016 Collection themed *Flowerland* Fendi has teamed up with Japanese botanical artist Azuma Makoto who created stun-ning installations at the brand's Ginza Pop-Up in Tokyo. Makoto converted a three-wheeled Piaggio Ape truck into a lush, foliage-covered mobile flower-shop displaying, among other things, tiny glass vessels filled with orchids and Fendi fur trimmings.

FENDI Ginza Pop-up Store, Tokyo

OLFACTIVE BRANDING

ANNA SINOFZIK—Culture Writer and Editor
Basend on an interview with Dawn Goldworm, Scent Director & Founder at 12.29

Smells can determine our moods and decisions. We famously follow our noses to instinctively sniff out the perfect partner. With signature fragrances filling the air of the world's sales rooms, we may now start sniffing out our favorite stores too.

We yearn to be rational when shopping, and yet we are largely led by emotions. Absorbed by store shelves stacked with visual attractions, we might not realize that our emotions are effectively triggered by scent. Smell sells, and even if the average customer is not overtly aware of this, businesses are, and increasingly they are using the promotional power of smell. They have a strong case: a few years ago, a study commissioned by Nike revealed that adding scents to the brand's retail environments increased the shoppers' intent to purchase by 80 percent. A series of gas stations in the U.S. reported a tripling of coffee purchases after the aroma of freshly ground beans had been pumped into the air near the fuel pumps, part of a test for a new type of scent-diffusing cannon.

Less brash than the latter example, many retail scents operate inconspicuously, subliminally even. "The emotional effect of smell is something most people are completely unaware of. In fact, few of us notice it being used at all," says custom scent specialist Dawn Goldworm. After working in the traditional perfume industry for a number of years, Goldworm now specializes in olfactive branding, and founded the firm 12.29 with her twin sister Samantha. The two work with clients such as Adidas, American Express, Mercedes Benz, Porsche, and Valentino, proving that scent can do a lot more than simply push sales.

If smell is the most emotive of the senses—as science corroborates—then scent can take the connection between brand and client to a whole new level, the Goldworms say. However, in a consumer world notoriously oversaturated with images and sounds, retailers have been relatively slow to tap into smell, says Steven Semoff, another scent specialist and former co-president of the Scent Marketing Institute. As *Adweek* reported a few years ago, global scent marketing has long been controlled by five companies from the U.S., who counted an estimated 10–20 percent of all North American retailers among their customers. Since the early nineties, when casino owners on the Sunset Strip found that scented slot machines could double their customers' stakes, ambient scenting has been widely used in stores, hotels, and gambling venues. And while it's catching on across airlines, funeral homes, retirement villages, medical practices, and law offices, scent branding as a transformational retail strategy is still in its infancy.

As the Goldworms state, they are among the first to offer custom fragrance as a mode of visceral storytelling—an approach that, in their experience, was first embraced by the creative industry. When they founded 12.29, they mainly scented fashion shows and art fairs: "Designers, creative directors, and artists appreciated the ability of scent to transform an experience," say the sisters. Unlike promotional air aromas, 12.29's scent identities are carefully crafted to be an integral part of the multisensory brand identity. Today, brands from various sectors striving to connect with their clientele through visceral storytelling commission 12.29 to develop scent identities for products, events, and retail environments.

"Olfactive science claims that 75 percent of our thoughts and moods are triggered by the smells that surround us," says Dawn Goldworm. "Scent and emotion live in the same part of the brain and directly influence one another. Thus, on a moment-to-moment basis, our emotions are literally being activated by our noses." Without detouring through the conscious-

"Bringing humanity back to experience through visceral connection, smell creates sales experiences that contemporary customers are searching for."

ness, a well-crafted custom scent can directly speak to our deepest feelings. Besides putting us in the mood to spend more, it can also make us linger longer and return to a store more regularly. It can enhance our perception of a retail experience—and of an entire brand.

Olfactive memories last, turning scent identities into powerful tools to build long-standing emotional loyalty. More effective than visuals or sounds, custom smells allow brands to build powerful connections that keep customers coming back. As studies confirm, we can remember smells with 65 percent accuracy after a year, while our visual recall is down to 50 percent after only three months. More effectively linked to the memory than any other sense, smell is also a force that can uncannily transport us back to the past. The emotional power of olfactive memory went down in cultural-scientific history as

Absorbed by store shelves stacked with visual attractions, we might not realize that our emotions are effectively triggered by scent.

the "madeleine moment," a term that refers to Marcel Proust's novel *À la recherche du temps perdu* (In Search of Lost Time) and its protagonist, who was transported back to his childhood after smelling a tea-soaked biscuit. Struck by a sudden sense of nostalgia, Proust's narrator notes: "When nothing else subsists from the past, after the people are dead, after the things are broken and scattered … the smell and taste of things remain poised a long time, like souls… bearing resiliently, on tiny and almost impalpable drops of their essence, the immense edifice of memory."

Impalpably and intricately tied up with individual memories, smells themselves are tricky to put into words—even for Proust, the so-called master of nuance. "The part of our brain that processes it is not connected to the part that comprehends and uses language," explains Goldworm. "That's why we can say we like a smell or not, but fail to describe it in detail." Dealing with the details of odors on a daily basis, Goldworm has developed the habit of turning to color to communicate with her clients. "Everyone around the world 'smells' the same colors. So when I am working with a brand, I can create the scent based on its tonality, such that anyone who experiences it associates the same tones, textures, and overall aesthetic atmosphere."

One of her all-time favorites is the scent identity 12.29 designed for Valentino, based on the fashion brand's iconic red, which they carefully crafted to symbolize its manifold facets. As the Goldworms put it in their portfolio: "The Valentino red is deep and intense. The Valentino red has a soft and warm texture that is light and transparent. The Valentino red is precise and timeless, laying close to the body. The Valentino red is a whisper that says I am effortless grace, simple beauty, and pure poetry." In order to translate their client's striking signature color into a custom

If smell is the most emotive of the senses—as science corroborates—then scent can take the connection between brand and client to a whole new level, the Goldworms say.

scent, the olfactive branding experts elaborated a blend of fresh germanium, delicate jasmine absolute, and precious amber, contrasted with accents of warm leather, patchouli, and fir balsam, deepening the tonality and adding a sense of softness to the otherwise vigorous flavor.

"While singular ingredients don't tell a story, a specific combination has the potential to transport us," Goldworm says. She compares the process of crafting a custom scent to the composition of colors in painting. One may also compare it to cooking. After all, taste is the sister sense of smell, the two closely connected. To return to Proust's madeleine, the taste of a tea-soaked biscuit is received into the olfactory system through buds in the back of our mouths, while its smell is taken up by nerves in the nasal area; our brain integrates both types of information. Whether we find a soggy biscuit delicate or gross is a different story.

"When still in the womb, we can smell what our mother is eating," Goldworm says. "This is the beginning of our taste preferences." While the French fondly dip their pastries into hot drinks, others prefer a crunchy cookie. Like all forms of taste, olfactive preferences are determined to a large degree by our sociocultural environment. But while our likings for visuals, sounds, or even foods tend to change throughout our lifetime based on ideas of belonging, identity, affiliation, or otherness, our taste for smell is more visceral, less able to be influenced, more deep-seated, and individually ingrained. "What scents appeal to us is largely based on what we experienced over the first 10 years of life," says Goldworm, pointing to the fact that Americans grow up with very different scentscapes than the Japanese, for example. "You really have to look into that to create a scent that resonates."

Apart from culture-specific influences, there are the highly individual ones of childhood memories. The Goldworms grew up in New Hampshire, naming the smell of

Like all forms of taste, olfactive preferences are determined to a large degree by our socio-cultural environment. But while our likings for visuals, sounds, or even foods tend to change throughout our lifetime, our taste for smell is more visceral.

the beach as one of their most profound olfactive memories. But as a professional nose knows, beaches smell differently in different parts of the world. As Dawn Goldworm describes, "the smell of United States' East Coast beaches is cold, salty, green, textured, and dry. During our childhood, it also had that touch of Hawaiian Tropic suntan lotion." Asked about other particularly long-lasting olfactive memories, she names the smell of a racetrack (her dad used to race cars) and that of Pond's Cold Cream (she was a ballet dancer for 13 years and used it to take off her stage makeup).

Dealing with the details of odors on a daily basis, Goldworm has developed the habit of turning to color to communicate with her clients.

It is due to individual experiences and associations like these that brands remain strangers to their target group's olfactive tastes. "There is no expression in our genes that says you will like this smell and not this one," explains Mark Peltier, president of a scent marketing firm called AromaSys, adding that certain universal indications can help scent specialists calculate the effect of an aroma. "Citrus smells are refreshing. Floral smells are relaxing. Herbaceous smells are usually relaxing but can also be invigorating, especially peppermint. Cedar and other wood smells relax and soothe." Patchouli, which formed part of 12.29's scent identity for Valentino, is said to have a grounding, balancing effect.

According to Goldworm, the success of a custom fragrance is all about the mix. The more multilayered a scent is, the smaller the risk of dropping the olfactive brick or of succumbing to stereotypes. In general, complex compositions also speak to broader target groups, and are therefore a crucial aspect when it comes to retail scents for global brands. While Valentino's stores do not smell different in Asia than they do in Europe or the U.S., the fragrance 12.29 developed for them is eclectic enough to connect to individuals from diverse cultural backgrounds. While never obviously identifiable in terms of ingredients and composition, a custom blend should strike a balance between discreet and distinctive. "We do not want to polarize the brand's clientele, but still need to ensure that we are catering to the target market's olfactive preferences," Goldworm says.

The latter is a matter of careful analysis. Like other aspects of branding, a custom scent can backfire if it does not correspond to the broader context. "Our process is based on a rigorous examination of the brand and its target markets, but it also closely relates to its existing, visual features," Scents that will be diffused into the air need to be carefully synchronized with the overall setting to evoke a consistent atmosphere. "There's a huge disconnect in your brain when a scent does not match the space," Goldworm notes.

Asked about the dos and don'ts of fragrances for retail spaces, Goldworm reveals that one of the most common mistakes is to go by the standards of a scent for skin. "We do not want people to feel as if they are walking into a wall of perfume," she says. It is again a matter of taste and target groups. But fashion brands, who like to scent a retail environment with their bestselling signature colognes or a custom air aroma based on them, can easily overdo it if they are not careful. About five years ago, Abercrombie & Fitch hit the headlines for dispersing their fragrance, Fierce, in extremely high concentrations

"Citrus smells are refreshing. Floral smells are relaxing. Herbaceous smells are usually relaxing but can also be invigorating, especially peppermint. Cedar and other wood smells relax and soothe."

into all of their stores. According to the brand, the strong "edgy" scent was particularly well received—both as a perfume, and in sales rooms. Eventually, it brought people to the streets to protest, as many claimed the chemicals in the scent threatened the health of the brand's employees and consumers while in-store. Others were merely annoyed by the smell.

Customers who visited Coco Chanel's first boutique in Paris on May 5, 1921, reputedly walked into a wall of perfume, too. A pioneer in many ways, the designer was also one of the first to scent a retail space

for promotional reasons. On the occasion of the launch of her iconic No. 5 scent, she instructed her staff to spray it all over the store, especially the dressing rooms and the entrance area, in order to draw customers in and push sales. Approximately 50 years later, some ambitious retailers began experimenting with the first scent diffusers. As Jennifer Dublino, COO of the Scent Marketing Institute, told *Adweek*, they used cartridges soaked in scented oil and a fan to blow it out." But while scents were really intense at first, they would soon wane. Today, technology allows retailers to distribute fragrances evenly and with precise control over their intensity. Those

Olfactive memories last, turning scent identities into powerful tools to build long-standing emotional loyalty.

willing to invest in the power of scent can integrate high-end diffusers into their stores' air-conditioning systems.

There is a somehow deceitful aftertaste when it comes to the use of custom scent as a means of customer manipulation. Unlike all other senses, we are unable to turn away from olfactive elements as they come through vent-mounted vaporizers. As Patrick Süskind put it in *Perfume*, we cannot escape scent, "for scent is the brother of breath." As mentioned earlier on, our sense of smell is directly linked to the brain's limbic system, such that olfactive information cannot be caught by the thalamus, which otherwise acts as a filter. While we have long learned how to block out a variety of visuals and sounds on our high streets, we are generally at the mercy of the smells that surround us. Goldworm notes that smell influences us to such a degree that even the U.S. military has used it as a tactic to scare off the enemy. However, she firmly dispels moral doubts. "The power of scent does not overtake all activities in the brain. It cannot take away free will."

Consumer weaponry rarely comes without critics, and in the battle for customers, smell is certainly something of a silver bullet. Applied scrupulously, it can help physical retail win back business. "Bringing humanity back to experience through visceral connection, smell creates sales experiences that contemporary customers are searching for," Goldworm concludes. With scientists eagerly working on the digitization of smells, online stores in a not too distant future may be scented, too. For now, scent remains one of the great opportunities for physical retail. And while there is no formula for the sweet smell of success, olfactive branding infuses a whiff of new optimism into brick-and-mortar sales. <

SIAM DISCOVERY

Offering customers a rich range of products at reasonable prices, the department store of the past anticipated e-commerce as we know it today. Commissioned by a Taiwanese development company, Japanese design firm Nendo has reimagined the classic retail concept while restoring a good deal of its former lure. The result is dubbed Siam Discovery. Conceived as an interactive "lifestyle laboratory," it celebrates the shopping experience beyond soulless click and buy.

The Siam Discovery retail complex gives new life to an 18-year-old, 40,000-square-meter building on Bangkok's Rama 1 thoroughfare, home to a former department store owned and managed by Taiwan's leading retail and real estate developers, Siam Piwat. With claims of setting new benchmarks in retail and always being one step ahead, the company has a track record of proposing successful prototypes of integrated retail and residential solutions. Mega-projects include ICONSIAM, an extensive estate that

spreads across 10 kilometers of Chao Phraya's riverbank. With Siam Discovery, the developers sought to blend a classic department store with the conceptual, narrative structure of a modern multi-brand boutique.

Led by a self-appointed mission to transform retail environments into holistic experiences that can excite and inspire, Siam Piwat wisely chose to collaborate with acclaimed design studio Nendo. "It was only Oki Sato and his team who I could imagine working with," says Chadatip Chutrakul, Siam Piwat's CEO, when thinking back on the project's planning phase. Nendo has a whimsical signature style that has shaped sculptural furniture pieces for manufacturers like Kartell and Cappellini, as well as offbeat in-store installations and interiors for clients such as Issey Miyake, Camper, Puma, and Starbucks. >

Entrance Hall

*Right_*The store's atrium is lined with 202 stacked box frames containing video displays that function as a directory for in-store events and merchandise.

*Below_*These stacked boxes are referenced in the design of the building's façade.

Nendo's creation turns shoppers into research fellows: roaming around test tubes, molecular side tables, and stalagmite stands, they find themselves probing a promising future for the physical store.

An avowed fan of the studio, Chutrakul encouraged the designers to eschew traditional department store categorizations. Instead of rows of racks organized by brands, she imagined an interactive narrative as a means to structure the retail center's five-story sales area. "Millennials are not addicted to brands," says Chutrakul. While some follow the Normcore fad of the purposely unfashionable, she argues that most are eager to support their strong sense of individuality through unique experiences. Drawing on observations like these, Siam Discovery invites a new generation of inquisitive shoppers to discover themselves and their unique needs amid a carefully curated selection of goods. "Customers who know what they want tend to buy online," notes Oki Sato, Nendo's founder. And as e-commerce offers efficiency through optimized search functions, brick-and-mortar stores stock up on ideas, unsuspected finds, and the certain, ungoogleable something.   >

Fragrances

Creativity and experimentation are recurring themes throughout the building. They are embodied in the beauty product displays shown here, which resemble laboratory-style steel-and-glass trolleys.

A Man's World

The merchandise is not arranged by brand but by lifestyle theme. Wares are displayed minimally on custommade displays, including trestle-style hanging rails and tables for casualwear and hundreds of stacking wooden crates for casual shoes.

Siam Piwat envisioned an interactive storytelling component here that would inspire the customers while putting their individual needs at the center. "Our role as a retailer has advanced from one of managing products, categories, and displays to one of managing visitors' experiences and emotions," explains Chutrakul. Running with the idea of a lifestyle laboratory, Nendo defined an overarching narrative that reflects the paradigm shift in physical retail: once essentially points of sale, today's stores serve to create the right chemistry between company and consumer.

Pleasantly poised between adventure playground and walk-in art installation, Siam Discovery brims with science-inspired props and an extensive range of custom-designed furniture that is worth a research trip alone. For the women's fashion area on the ground floor, Nendo designed 20 different tables and stands inspired by molecular structures and diagrams. One flight up, in the menswear department, one finds carefully crafted shoe pedestals in the twisted shape of the DNA helix. In the eyewear >

> **"Our role as a retailer has advanced from one of managing products, categories, and displays to one of managing visitors' experiences and emotions."—Chadatip Chutrakul, CEO, Siam Piwat**

Ladies department

*Above_*A curated selection of footwear is displayed on countless circular plinths that form a monochrome marble landscape.

*Right_*Fitting rooms line a spacious gallery that is reminiscent of a glasshouse, with an elaborate metal-frame structure and mirrors instead of glass.

department, columnar product displays and lamps permeate space like stalagmites and stalactites permeate caves. The "Digital Lab" displays technical gadgets on luminous, giant microscope lenses. And back down on the ground floor, in the "Skin Lab," cosmetics and fragrances can be tested on a large surgical table.

As customers move through the departments of Siam Discovery, Chutrakul says they are "drawn into stories relevant to their interests," adding that the retail concept offers plenty of opportunities to personalize purchases. Most importantly, it encourages customers to engage with the space and its products. A prime example of experiential retail, Nendo's >

Siam Discovery invites a new generation of inquisitive shoppers to discover themselves and their unique needs amid a carefully curated selection of goods.

creation turns shoppers into research fellows: roaming around test tubes, molecular side tables, and stalagmite stands, they find themselves probing a promising future for the physical store.

Of course, an increase in customer traffic is the most immediate objective of every experiential retail space. Nendo's design process began with a challenge in this respect, as a particularly narrow façade reduced the flow of visitors entering at the front. To solve this problem, the designers connected several existing atriums and created an inviting, open space that extends toward the back of the > building. Sato describes it as a canyon-like structure, imposing enough to attract pedestrians and guide them well inside the store. He wanted visitors to look straight up and get the overall picture upon entering the space, and also a sense of what to expect on the upper floors, adding a four-story-high display wall. Stacked with 202 frame-shaped boxes that can be used as video monitors, for digital signage, and as merchandise displays, the multimedia floor plan functions as a directory, designed to draw people in. "By repositioning the escalators to run through the >

Pure Elegance

*Above_*In the homeware department, rows of light fittings resemble scientific flasks and funnels.

*Left_*In the women's fashion area, geometric forms give shape to the custom-made furniture, providing quirky cone-shaped pedestals in neutral colors.

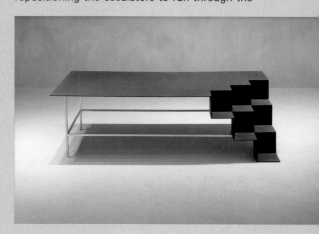

In the eyewear department, columnar product displays and lamps permeate space like stalagmites and stalactites permeate caves.

atrium and wall, we also facilitated a smooth flow of visitors throughout the building," adds Sato.

Extending from the first floor to the fifth, from common areas to the client-curated retail spaces, the design of Siam Discovery marks Nendo's most extensive project thus far. The conception of the complete redevelopment plan, which included both the interior and exterior renovation of the large-scale complex, stretched over the course of one year, with a second one needed to turn it into reality. The award-winning result is, above all, characterized by an atmosphere "where people can feel relaxed and free to approach the products," finds Sato. As a designer, he believes the comfort factor is key—in all areas of his multi-faceted practice. "In the end, it really doesn't make a big difference for me if I design chewing gum packaging or a huge retail environment," he concludes. "It's always about giving small smiles to people." <

Accessories

Optical illusion is a common theme and lends a sense of exploration. In the eyewear corner, items are displayed on jet-black columns thrusting up from the floor. Mirrored by columns jutting down from the ceiling, they appear to float in space.

LUXURY BRAND NARRATIVES AND ARCHITECTURE

DORON BEUNS—Artist & Author of The Architectural Incarnation of Luxury Fashion Brands

Luxury retail is about more than expensive, well-crafted, and prestigious products. It is about the consumer's desire for new experiences that luxury brands must provide in their flagship stores. These stores offer the best service and widest range of products, and they are created with the goal of evoking all the aesthetic, symbolic, and functional benefits of the respective luxury brand.

Every benefit should become tangible, physical, and interactive within the flagship store. Marketing scholars Glyn Atwal and Alistair Williams have labelled this marketing strategy "experiential marketing."

This trend has been widely adopted in the realm of retail and has inspired an ongoing collaboration between architects, interior designers, and luxury fashion houses. One of the first luxury brands to leverage experiential retail was Prada. In 2001, the Italian label commissioned architect Rem Koolhaas to design its NYC Prada Epicenter, an experimental retail concept that combines an exclusive boutique, public space, and gallery in a 23,500-square-foot space that formerly belonged to the Guggenheim Museum. However, this pioneering act was not without flaws: a quarter of the 40-million-dollar budget was invested into automated dressing-room doors, microclimate systems, and touchscreens that either malfunctioned or were ignored by consumers.

Nevertheless, many luxury brands followed Prada's lead and have enlisted the help of renowned architects like Peter Marino and Gwenael Nicolas. A collaboration with well-known architects underlines the importance that luxury companies place on the physical representation of their brand. Each flagship store is a tangible manifestation of the respective brand's values, vision, and heritage and thus features aesthetic, symbolic, and functional brand references in the retail space. Long-lasting traditions, upon which so many brand narratives rely, become cutting-edge through

retail design. In the following three case studies of luxury fashion flagship stores, I will define the contemporary design components that represent the aesthetic, symbolic, and functional aspects of each respective brand. The case studies demonstrate different retail design approaches in three parts of the world and describe the elements that constitute a luxury fashion flagship store today. The first case study is Fendi's flagship store in Rome, located in an eighteenth-century palazzo that has been refurbished by Gwenael Nicolas. The store also houses a VIP space, a hotel with seven suites, and an award-winning Japanese restaurant. The second case study is Dior's flagship store in Seoul, designed by Peter Marino and located in a building by architect Christian de Portzamparc. The store includes a rooftop café that serves desserts by French pastry chef Pierre Hermé. The last case study will look at the Louis Vuitton flagship store in Los Angeles, fully designed by architect Peter Marino. This store does not include any secondary businesses but does have a private shopping suite for VIP customers on its third floor.

The Façade

Flagship stores may have extraordinary services but it is primarily their aesthetics that create brand-specific experiences for customers. This first impression of a brand's aesthetics occurs the moment a consumer views the façade of their flagship store. The colors, materials, and form of the façade reflect the ethos and most iconic products of the luxury fashion house.

Fendi's eighteenth-century palazzo signifies the brand's Roman origin and symbolically reflects its mission to preserve tradition. The beige hue of Palazzo Fendi aesthetically echoes the brand's iconic neutral-color leather goods from 1933. This reference can also be seen in the warm glow that illuminates the building's windows and celebrates Fendi's use of vivid color across the entire collection.

The Louis Vuitton flagship in Beverly Hills takes the form of a modern, silver box that has the mechanical capacity to open itself up to light. The shape of the flagship store alludes to Louis Vuitton's iconic travel trunks, which have been carefully crafted since the early nineteenth century. The way the building's surface opens and closes to light nods to the opening and closing of a trunk during one's travels. These two architectural elements symbolically refer to the brand's heritage as a supplier of fine travel accessories.

The spectacular façade of Dior's flagship store in Seoul consists of a vertical, curved silhouette that is made of fiberglass panels. The color and construction of the building are reminiscent of Dior's white toile fabrics that have been seamed together in the brand's tailoring atelier. The curvilinear form can be traced back to designer Christian Dior's iconic 1950s New Look. This reference becomes even more apparent when including the small pagoda-style roof, which is the architectural equivalent of the hat that topped off his New Look. Another significant aspect of the flagship store is the steel reinforcement that subtly reveals itself at the arched entrance and signifies the functional relation between Dior's bell-shaped designs and their reinforced fabrics. Behind the curved façade, a cubical counterpart houses the menswear department. The surface of the cube is engraved with the cannage pattern that is often used to brand Dior's leather goods. The signature pattern also once adorned the wicker chairs at Dior's headquarters at

32 Avenue Montaigne in Paris. A star on top of this cubical structure references the good fortune of founder Christian Dior. Finally, there is significance to the scale and placement of the Seoul flagship store: it resembles the townhouse-like scale and corner placement of Dior's original Paris headquarters on the intersection of Avenue Montaigne and Rue François.

The Shop Floor

Once the customer is lured by the impressive appearance of the façade, they enter the shop's selling floor. This is where products are displayed and aesthetic, symbolic, and functional references reinforce the brand's identity.

The shop floor of Palazzo Fendi is characterized by the dominance of beige tones that aesthetically reference Fendi's naturally hued leather accessories from 1933. Touches of marble, limestone, and silver can be perceived as opulent references to ancient Rome. The irregular coloration, structure, and shimmer of these materials is reminiscent of fur, a recurring fabric in Fendi's fashion and accessory collections. The shifting, vertical, and rectangular shapes of product displays nod to the double letter F in the Fendi logo. The strict geometry of the logo is also reflected by the angular lines of the ceiling and the black graphic lines on the floor and furniture frames.

When stepping into the Louis Vuitton flagship store the customer sees the box shape of a Louis Vuitton trunk represented in the rectangular pattern of the floor, the cubically shaped furniture, and the rectangular furniture. The partially open and partially covered constructions of the shop's displays reinforce the association of opening and closing a Louis Vuitton trunk. Another iconic aspect of the brand that is reflected in the interior is the Damier check pattern. Its brown and beige tones repeat in the floor, carpet, table, and chairs. However, the rhythm of the pattern inside the store has more variance than the original template and creates a sense of motion. This feeling of movement is reinforced through the irregular textures of the curved chairs, light brown carpet, and store display. Although the fashion house has long since extended their product range, the concept

of travel remains at the heart of the brand and serves as the underlying theme for the retail experience in Louis Vuitton stores.

Upon entering Dior's flagship store in Seoul, the customer cannot help but notice the dominance of the color gray and the Louis XV medallion-shaped chairs and chandeliers. Both elements are aesthetic references to the wall color and furniture in Christian Dior's original Parisian headquarters. A variation of the legendary cannage pattern can be found in the vertical, horizontal, and diagonal lines in the black ecru floor pattern, which also resembles the color combination of Dior's original New Look. However, Christian Dior was not always a legendary fashion designer—he once co-owned an art gallery. This previous career is symbolically referenced by a suspended sculpture by Korean artist Lee Bul. And the small glittering lights in the ceiling that resemble stars signify the designer's belief that he was always destined for success.

The Transit Spaces

Transit spaces, such as the foyer and the staircase, are areas of a flagship store where no products are on display. Nevertheless, the architect must ensure that distinguishing elements of the respective luxury brand are still present.

The foyer of Fendi's flagship store recalls the Roman heritage of the brand. Materials such as dark red marble and travertine limestone allude to ancient Rome. This is complemented by eighteenth-century palazzo arches that bulge from the light beige walls. The red marble staircase also nods to Roman history with a design that is inspired by the renaissance architecture of Giacomo Barozzi da Vignola. The veining of the marble mimics the coloration, shimmer, and texture of fur. And the extravagant presence of precious stones and silver ceilings reflect the lavishness of Fendi's fur and leather goods.

The transition spaces of the Louis Vuitton LA store include aesthetic elements that reference Louis Vuitton's iconic trunks and Damier pattern. White wall panels with transparent counterparts offer a variation on the signature check. The interplay of opacity and transparency repeats on the edge of the mezzanine, once again referring to the opening and closing

of Louis Vuitton's trunks. The brand's iconic trunks are presented on wall displays as sculptural stacks. Opposite these stacks, a pink sculpture by Los Angeles artist Aaron Curry symbolizes Louis Vuitton's historical ties to the art world and positions the trunk as a well-crafted work of art in its own right.

The staircase area in Dior's Seoul flagship store illustrates the importance of nature as a source of inspiration for the brand. Eight porthole video installations, projecting blue splashes of seawater, refer to the Norman Sea near Christian Dior's childhood villa. They also symbolize the designer's previously mentioned relationship to the art world and represent his lucky number: eight. According to Peter Marino, the staircase itself resembles an unfurling ribbon, which is a metaphor for Dior's feminine designs and the decorations that are applied to them in the atelier floor. When walking up the stairs, the view reveals the aerial perspective of a rose, one of the many flowers that was found in Christian Dior's childhood garden and inspired his designs.

These three case studies demonstrate how interior designers and architects draw inspiration from a fashion label's heritage to create a retail environment that serves as a contemporary manifestation of the brand story. Various design elements create a constant interplay between aesthetic, symbolic, and functional references. Some elements serve as strong individual symbols, while others only become meaningful within particular groupings. A well-designed luxury fashion flagship store creates as much of an impact on a broader, conceptual level as it does with its details. Some customers spend hours in a flagship store and although the multiple layers of meaning may not reveal themselves to everyone, they leave their mark on the mind of the consumer and are thus essential for the brand narrative to be perpetuated. <

Flagship stores may have extraordinary services but it is primarily their aesthetics that create brand-specific experiences for customers.

JARDAN Flagship Store

Using Sydney's sun-bleached colors as a back-drop, Melbourne-based firm IF ARCHITECTURE seeks to promote Jardan's furniture by selling a lifestyle to go with it.

For the last three decades, Jardan has designed and manufactured all of their modernist-inspired furniture and lighting in Melbourne, crafting their wares from locally sourced woods and textiles to the highest environmental standards. Their ethos is to make products that are loved and lived with, and that grow and change with families over generations. The team at IF Architecture took this to heart when designing their flagship store in Sydney, which opened in 2017. They took inspiration from the colors and moods of the work of the city's most influential art-world families, as well as from Brett Whiteley and Marion Hall Best. With natural light flooding in from a giant skylight, the emphasis here is on color. Subtle transitions between whites, blues, greens, pink, grays, and blacks shift the mood as you walk from one room to the next. The result: walking the floors of this store with its standout sculptural staircase feels more like taking a tour of a family home than visiting a showroom. <

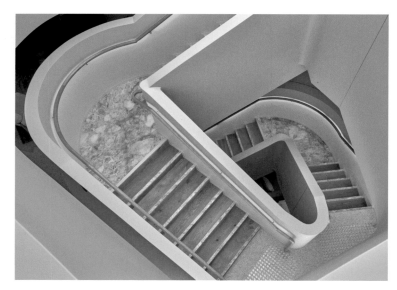

There is an emphasis on color throughout the Jardan store. Specifically, IF Architects has created a system of color that plays with shifts in a customer's mood, transitioning between levels as he or she walks through the showroom.

NIRAV MODI Flagship Store

Elegance, playfulness, and innovation are all buzzwords that describe Spanish artist-designer JAIME HAYON's exquisite design for Nirav Modi's eponymous flagship jewelry store. Set within 1,830 square meters, over two floors, his installation-like approach truly dazzles.

Nirav Modi founded his global diamond jewelry house in 2010. One of several generations of diamantaires, Modi counts Kate Winslet, Rosie Huntington-Whiteley, Naomi Watts, and Coco Rocha among his prestigious clientele. Stepping into his retail store, which opened in 2014 in the upmarket Defence Colony area of New Delhi, is like walking into the most luxuriant, felt-lined jewelry box filled with gems in the most exquisite forms. Jaime Hayon has created a precious environment in which attention to detail is bound with the craftsmanship of a series of showcase installations. The custom-designed furniture includes highly lacquered tables and plush seating with brass trim. Everything sparkles and shines against a backdrop of jet black and soft dove gray. And the prolific use of mirrored walls and ceilings takes the design to a new level that is at once dynamic, enchanting, and mesmerizing—like the jewelry on display. <

In the River Room, customers perch alongside a marble countertop that nearly fills the space. Here, as elsewhere in the store, eye-catching, custom-designed furniture made from the most luxurious of materials captures the exquisite charm of the jewels on display.

SALLE PRIVÉE Milan Showroom

To create the striking design of Salle Privée's House No. 8 in Milan, Rotterdam-based Studio SABINE MARCELIS drew inspiration from the store's original sixteenth-century interior. The concept, like the brand it showcases, seamlessly blends contemporary style with timeless elegance.

Salle Privée is a Dutch menswear label that prides itself on creating a classic range of clothing and accessories. Its iconic designs focus on comfort and style and are made by Italian firms using the highest-quality materials. The brand's Milan store, House No. 8, occupies a space in the handsome Palazzo Recalcati, a sixteenth-century building on Via Amedei in the heart of the city. Many of the building's architectural and decorative features have been preserved over the centuries, and Studio Sabine Marcelis used them to develop an interior that combines futuristic details with elements from the past. For example, a rich marble floor mirrors the original, ornately painted domed ceiling, and the space between is dominated by modern plexiglass structures. Cutout shapes in the plexiglass reflect those in the ceiling decoration, creating a harmonious feel that marries sixteenth-century architecture with twenty-first-century technology. This concept embodies contemporary style and timeless elegance, phrases that capture the ethos of the luxury menswear on display. <

DOLCE & GABBANA Flagship Store

With an impressive series of palatial rooms, all sumptuously outfitted by Japan's CURIOSITY Architectural Studio, the Dolce & Gabbana flagship store in Milan is the epitome of the brand's dynamic personality.

The walls of the Dolce & Gabbana flagship store are lined with striking panels of book-matched green marble and onyx. The shop's fitting rooms and alcoves are dressed in richly figured, highly polished walnut. Smooth matte-black lava stone floors are graced with carpets of shimmering gold. Curiosity Architectural Studio's concept awakens curiosity as it seeks to connect Dolce & Gabbana's past with its present through design that combines the energy of the baroque with the clarity of modernism. Above each room, bright lights are set within a high-tech ceiling to highlight the garments and accessories on display below. Gilded furnishings feel fit for royalty with plush upholstery in masculine peacock-blue and sage-green tones, while luxuriant damask wallpapers bring a welcome softness that is echoed in the elegant lines of the clothing. With huge ceiling mirrors doubling the effect, Curiosity's design encapsulates not only the luxury of this Italian fashion house but also the timeless sophistication of its creations. <

The marbling of the precious stones enters into a delicate interplay with light as the consumer moves through the space, creating a certain sense of suspense and drama that is part of Dolce & Gabbana's DNA. For Gwenael Nicolas, the founder and chief designer at Curiosity, it is exactly this sensation a customer is experiencing while moving through the shop that forms an integral part of the overall design.

ENES Concept Store

Dutch fashion store Enes celebrates 15 years with a maximalist design from interior designer GERT VOORJANS. The Belgian stamps his inimitable style on a four-story lifestyle store in which you can shop, drink, and even sleep.

Enes sells an assortment of women's clothing, hand-picked from a wide variety of domestic and foreign labels. To celebrate the brand's 15th anniversary, founder Muriel Van Nieuwenhove enlisted the services of Belgian designer Gert Voorjans, who created an experiential space within a historic townhouse on Antwerp's Volkstraat. With this project, Van Nieuwenhove was looking to not only expand her range to include a selection of jewels, homeware, books, and magazines, but also to develop the building's top two floors into a guesthouse. Voorjans's flamboyant style is wholly in tune with the brand's eclectic flair, making for a perfect mix of period art nouveau features with bright pops of color that include a Coca-Cola-red jewelry display counter and bold leaf-print fabrics. In addition to clothing displays, customers can browse a wood-paneled bathroom stocked with skin care products, and a specially fitted original Cubex kitchen showcasing one-off objects curated by Van Nieuwenhove. When it's time to take a rest from shopping, visitors can sit back and soak up the heady atmosphere in the cozy Enes bar. <

Voorjans has created a series of intimate spaces within the store. Each one reflects a distinct domestic theme. Skin care products are stocked in a wood-paneled bathroom, while clothes are displayed in rooms with a private, dressing-room ambience.

HERMÈS

Known for the unmatched quality of its products and the skills of its expert master craftsmen, Hermès is a world reference when it comes to the timelessness of its savoir faire. Protective of its past and yet innovative in its approach to creativity, the luxury house has a unique way of staging its creations by opening its doors to whimsical worlds and dreamscapes.

"Our Maison's history, and legacy, are rooted in the work of master craftsmen, artisans, and artists," explained Pierre-Alexis Dumas, Hermès's artistic director, during his inaugural speech at the opening of Maison Hermès in Shanghai (2014). "Like a tree, we rely on our roots—our strength—to grow; every season, we imagine creative collections that branch out." If Hermès's core expertise and precious craft have been passed along for generations through its different ateliers, the luxury brand also knows how to venture out and explore new paths. Atelier petit h, for example, has been exemplary in the way it pushes craftsmanship in new directions. >

Hermès à tire-d'aile – Les mondes de Leïla Menchari
Exhibition at Grand Palais, Paris, 2017

*Below_* Leïla Menchari fashioned many exquisite scenes for Hermès between 1978 and 2013. Masterful with color and a doyenne of creating fantasy, Menchari used an eclectic range of props to display Hermès's luxury wares. She was key in establishing the design of the window display as an art form in itself at Hermès, a tradition the Maison has adopted for all its boutiques around the world and that now forms an integral part of the brand.

*Opposite_* The storefront of the historical Faubourg Saint-Honoré store in Paris.

Experience driven, Hermès's retail offer becomes more and more staged like an exhibition, always staging the unexpected to create a surprise.

Window displays at Faubourg Saint-Honoré Store, Paris

By Antoine Platteau

Antoine Platteau became Leïla Menchari's successor in designing the window displays of the brands' legendary flagship store at Rue du Faubourg Saint-Honoré. His interpretations of the fashion house's rich visual universe result in graphic and poetic sceneries that are deeply influenced by his background as a cinema scenographer and decorator.

Opposite page_Christmas Delight, Window by Antoine Platteau for Faubourg Saint-Honoré Store, Christmas 2017

Above left_Spring is just around the corner, Window by Antoine Platteau for Faubourg Saint-Honoré Store, Spring 2015

Above right_Patience et longueur de temps..., Window by Antoine Platteau for Faubourg Saint-Honoré Store, Fall 2015

Right_Métamorphose de la matière, First window by Antoine Platteau for Faubourg Saint-Honoré Store, Spring 2014

The Hand

Physiologically, the hand is composed of five fingers, and craftsmanship has always revolved around the hand's ability to create, shape, and invent. Beyond its power as a tool, the hand is linked to a person's vision, the thought process behind the eventual object. If the hand won't change, the vision will. From the start, Hermès's petit h ateliers aimed at triggering creative thinking outside of the box. Our era is bringing countless changes. Compared to our ancestors, this generation is confronted with a new world order where globalization, togetherness, and new kinds of intelligence foster collaborations. A respect for heritage and the transmission of values still command the hand, but the context has shifted: these younger craftsmen have gained independence from the weight of the past. They are on the lookout for new expressions and genres; they transcend frontiers by integrating cutting-edge technologies or opening up to new savoir faire. Decades ago, in rural areas, a blacksmith would not know about the intricate work of the lacemaker living nearby, nor encounter her. There is endless potential in cross-referencing craftsmanship(s), and that is precisely what petit h builds its knowledge and expertise on.

Today, Hermès sees the benefits of bringing together artisans from various fields. A master glassmaker will passionately spend hours unearthing a design process with a master silversmith and a master saddler. Every time craftsmen collaborate, the object they create pushes boundaries; what's more, it crystallizes shared experience(s). These >

Rue de Sèvres Store, Paris

By RDAI

For the brand's first boutique on the Left Bank of Paris, design group RDAI made a conscious effort to conserve and reinterpret the architecture of the former swimming pool building in which the store is housed. The interior design features beautifully sculptural display structures made from laths of ash. Each of these nine-meter-high wooden pavilions features a different Hermès collection and creates a sense of intimacy within the spacious interior.

As the brand explores novel ways for brand expression, new forms of retail emerge: there is less to buy and more to look at or learn from at Hermès's stores today.

shared experiences are an integral part of Hermès's DNA today: as the brand reaches new corners of the world, it calls for more and more creativity within its stores, pop-up events, and retail experiences.

As the brand explores novel ways for brand expression, new forms of retail emerge: there is less to buy and more to look at or learn from at Hermès's stores today. Experience-driven, Hermès's retail offer becomes more and more like an exhibition, always staging the unexpected to create a surprise. Whimsical worlds and dreamscapes speak to the child in us, and turn the colors of our dreams into key visual elements in the brand's retail spaces. For example, in the Paris flagship, located in a listed 1935 art deco building on Rue de Sèvres, one walks into a vast oblong space designed by RDAI (the firm responsible for the architecture of all Hermès stores across the world), where three huts rise nine meters high from the spacious central sunken area, down from the ground floor. Each one, built from 270 unique strips of curving ash wood, resonates with a primitive yet utterly modern feel. The intertwined structures have a nomadic lightness and subtly hint at Hermès's beloved art of travel. Grown-up fairytale magic instantly activates.

The Wings of Storytelling

Whether it is to fly higher or escape the mundane, wings are a recurrent metaphor in Hermès's visual language: Pegasus, the divine, winged stallion, floats above the historical Parisian flagship and *les ailes d'Hermès* (literally, the wings of Hermès) is the name given to the company's creative online portal (lesailes.hermes.com). Dreaming, spreading one's artistic wings, reaching for the skies—such are the messages encrypted in Hermès's creative DNA. It therefore comes as no surprise that Leïla >

Hermèsmatic

In 2016, Hermès launched a pop-up concept called *Hermèsmatic*. Featuring washing machines in the brand's signature orange hue, the store offered a dip-dyeing service to customers, free of charge, to give old scarves a new lease of life in fuschia, violet, or denim blue. Having toured several major cities since its launch, *Hermèsmatic* is not only an eye-catching installation that sparks media buzz, but also an excellent example of how a brand can reconnect with its customer base, by offering an innovative service.

Menchari's retrospective exhibition at Le Grand Palais was named *"Hermès à tire d'aile, les mondes de Leïla Menchari"* (Hermès in a Dashing Flight). From 1978 until 2013, Menchari designed the house's windows on Rue du Faubourg Saint-Honoré; with flair and talent, she worked with countless craftsmen to imagine giant waves sculpted out of marble, fantasy Kelly bags made out of metal, multicolored saddles with wings, and a Paris-themed window with monuments in organza. Menchari's work was all about storytelling.

"Leïla, an admirer of Dalí and the surrealists, discovered that 'in the Hermès workshops, anything is possible.' Including making her dreams reality," explained Axel Dumas, Hermès's chief executive officer, at the opening of the exhibition (2017). "Elation, and dizziness: when reality can be raised to the level of dream, when the magic works, the challenge is to repeat the trick, which means constantly feeding and irrigating the wonder, raising the level of delight, spurring the imagination to be endlessly creative: audacious, in a word. And, at the same time, the result had to be impeccable: there was no room for approximation. (…) When designing a scene, there must always be some mystery, for mystery is an invitation to fill in the gaps left by the imagination." It is with this deeply rooted ethos in mind that Hermès consistently creates enchanting retail spaces. And regardless of whether they appear in airports, boutiques, or flagship stores, Hermès's windows never disappoint. Always inventive, they showcase >

Every opening of a Hermès Maison is a new statement on creativity, architecture, art, and design. For its first Maison in China, Hermès chose the former French Concession in Shanghai.

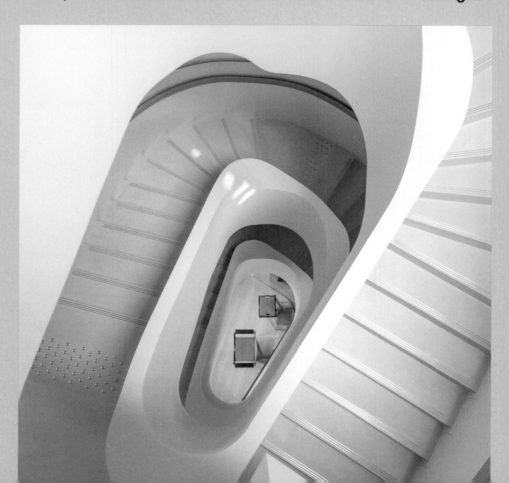

Maison Shanghai

By RDAI

Launched in 2014, the Hermès Maison in Shanghai is located in a historic brick building that has served both as a school and as a police station in the past. With the opening of the store coinciding with the Chinese year of the horse, Hermès seized the opportunity to host a temporary exhibition on the creature, which is a key visual element for the brand as it points to its origins as a saddle-maker.

Museum of Supernatural History, Maison Shanghai

By Zim & Zou

Zim & Zou's *Museum of Supernatural History* (2015) was inspired by nature, with two windows focusing on air and water and two on earth. A 16-foot paper plesiosaur fossil dominates the tripartite water window, cruising above cabinets filled with Hermès curiosities in subtle underwater-world shades.

As the brand reaches new corners of the world, it calls for more and more creativity within its stores, pop-up events, and retail experiences.

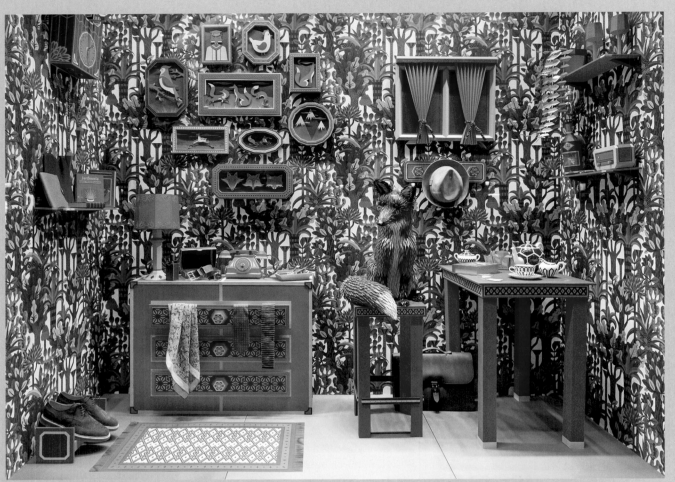

**Whether it is in a flagship store or a corner shop at the airport—
Hermès's windows never disappoint. Always inventive, they showcase
young, independent talents that range from scenographers to artists,
designers to craftsmen.**

young, independent talents that range from scenographers to artists, designers to craftsmen. And more
importantly, Hermès does so locally, sourcing regional talents to contextualize the brand's aspirations.

Other pop-up experiences, like Hermèsmatic,
travel the world to encounter different audiences.
The idea behind this project is a tongue-in-cheek
experiment that aims to give any Hermès scarf a
bold second life. Picture a large orange laundromat
bedecked with the Hermès logo in New York with full-
size orange washing machines lined up against the
wall. Standing in front, dye experts inspect the nature
and quality of twill silk scarves. The good candidates
are then eligible for a complete make-over (or wash-
over, rather) in bolder colors.

petit h

A one-of-a-kind creative endeavor, atelier petit h is
the brainchild of Pascale Mussard, great-great-grand-
daughter of Thierry Hermès. So, what happens at petit
h? Under Mussard's guidance, a team of hand-picked
black-belt artisans use the leftover materials from the
Hermès manufacturing process, and transform them >

HERMÈS *The Fox's Den,* Barcelona Paseo de Gracia store & *Forest Folks,* Dubai Mall of the Emirates

into, well, anything—as long as the finished product is functional. In Mussard's petit h, the craftsmen simply become laboratory scientists. The concept of petit h, after all, could be summed up as an atelier that preserves the craft and pushes innovation.

Therefore, collaborations between petit h and designers have always been bold. Take Faye Toogood's vibrant red conceptual installation that filled the ground floor of London's Bond Street flagship in 2013. For the store's opening, Studio Toogood created red structures using a blown-up template of a Hermès bag. "The piece that caught my eye was a leather off-cut of a signature Hermès bag pattern," said Faye Toogood. "The hide was a skeleton of the negative shapes left by the pattern cutters who had cut the intricate shapes. It was so inspiring for me to work within such an established house, with strong codes, and be encouraged in finding beauty in the unexpected." The creative scenography further expressed how the brand "relentlessly pushes the boundaries of craftsmanship and materials," said Toogood. Yet another petit h collaboration went in the same direction, with designers Nicolas Daul and Julien Demanche revisiting terrazzo tiles, incrusting small Hermès metal spare parts like locks, rivets, or tiny keys inside the material.

Slow Culture

Every opening of a Hermès Maison is a new statement on creativity, architecture, art, and design. For its first Maison in China, Hermès chose the former French Concession in Shanghai. At night, the heritage brick façade evokes a classic quattrocento >

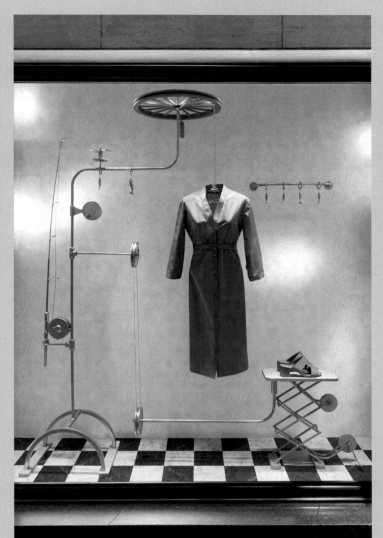

Contraptions, **London Bond Street Store**

By StoreyStudio

There is an air of eccentric invention in StoreyStudio's 2017 window displays for the brand's London store, in which heritage sporting goods are displayed amid madcap brass contraptions. The design awakens the curiosity of the passer-by, encouraging him or her to explore the unique qualities of each product.

**Window Display,
Stockholm Store**

By Joann Tan Studio

The Joann Tan Studio created these two window displays for the Hermès store in Stockholm.

*Opposite_* For the *Hermès Cats* theme, the designers used cats on the prowl to conjure an atmosphere of urban exploration.

*Above_* For the *Hermès Art* theme, the designers came up with the original concept of Hermès trademark silk scarves emerging from tubes of paint in the brand's colors and patterns.

palace, while the reflective ponds on each side of the entrance create a moment of tranquillity for visitors to the space, a former school turned police station originally built in 1928.

The 1,170-square-meter store, more than six years in the making, is something of a metaphor for Hermès's steady, unhurried approach to China. "Heritage and quality, enhanced with modernity and creativity, will be the keys to Hermès's success in China," affirmed Weiming Cao, the company's president for Greater China since late 2013, at the opening of Maison Hermès in Shanghai (2014). "In China, we

want to promote the 'hand' and Hermès's slow culture for exceptional objects," he continued. "We believe it will prove the best strategy in the long run. We expect a healthy growth, based on the intrinsic quality of the objects we craft. Historically, China has been a country of craftsmanship: craft was a traditional pillar before the Cultural Revolution. Today, this consciousness is on the rise again."

On the second floor of the new Shanghai store, one finds three expert ateliers dedicated to leather, tailoring, and watchmaking. "We welcome customers to see, feel, touch, and exchange with our >

Dreaming, spreading one's artistic wings, reaching for the skies—such are the messages encrypted in Hermès's creative DNA.

dedicated craftsmen," says Cao. "Our stores can be compared to editorials and our store directors to editors-at-large: each boutique, or Maison, reflects their personality, their understanding and vision for the local market."

   "Working with visionaries, one understands that there is a common language; a universality in working with the hand," added Pascale Mussard while unveiling a petit h collection in New York inside the Hermès flagship (2016). She could never take her eyes off the hands of craftsmen around her; she also found them hardened by labor, by "gestures that people have done since man was born. Our generation forgot a little bit of that, and we have to react." For Mussard, luxury means taking time to practice and appreciate craft, to respect experience in praise of know-how, with an open-minded approach to creativity.   <

The City Awakens, Stockholm Store

By Joann Tan Studio

In Joann Tan Studio's window displays entitled *The City Awakens,* for Hermès's Stockholm store in 2015, the designer presents some typically Parisian urban scenes in which the city comes alive. Each building has a personality of its own, with windows that become winking eyes and doors that mouth greetings. Various items from the accessories collection adorn the buildings, transforming them into the main protagonists of city life. The Arc de Triomph yawns sleepily into a leather glove and a streetlight is draped in a jaunty scarf.

HERMÈS *The City Awakens* Window Display, Stockholm Store

BEEHIVE Fashion Store

Celebrated American interior designer DUFFY STONE conjures up an interior for the Beehive fashion boutique that is awash with sunset hues. An emphasis on the tropical immediately transports customers to a sunny beach.

Oversized Monstera leaves and lush palm fronds grace a feature wall in this independent boutique dedicated to hip, young women's fashion. The plants set a tropical tone that instantly marries with the lilac, tangerine, and peach shades that dominate the space. Renowned for her bold use of color, interior designer Duffy Stone does not disappoint at the Beehive fashion boutique. The palette hints at the perfect sunset and lends a spirit of vacation adventure that is only intensified by the colonial-style faux-cane chairs and a bejeweled Chinese umbrella. The cohesive interior combines clothing displays with a boudoir-style seating area and a run of changing rooms. There is a distinct lack of formality here, with a mellow color scheme, soft rugs, and plush velvet lounge chairs enhancing the brand's laid-back vibe. One thing is for sure: the sun always shines at the Beehive. <

BEEHIVE Fashion Store

SÉ ENSEMBLE Showroom

Luxury furniture brand Sé created the Sé Ensemble mini-apartment for Milan Design Week with a flair and ethos that matches its vision. The result is a haven of craftsmanship, curvaceousness, and timelessness complete with flowers, fragrance, and music.

Founded in 2007 by Pavlo Schtakleff, Sé is at the forefront of contemporary luxury furniture design. Working with the world's best design talent, the brand's catalog of highly crafted and beautifully finished objects is made of the finest, most opulent materials: plush upholstery, polished marble, and rich brass tones. Set within the atmospheric Galleria Rossana Orlandi for Milan Design Week 2017, the Sé Ensemble featured a mini-apartment with a lounge, a dining room, a dressing room, and a salon. Presented with rugs from French producer La Manufacture Cogolin and artisanal wallpapers by Brooklyn-based Calico, new pieces from selected artists, sculptors, and craftsmen created a diverse mix of pattern, texture, and shape. By placing their works in this unique apartment context, Sé was able to demonstrate the adaptability of its brand. <

Pieces from the three collections that Sé has launched since its 2007 founding are distributed among the four rooms of the exhibit. The products presented include those by Spanish designer Jaime Hayon and Slovenian designer Nika Zupanc.

SÉ ENSEMBLE Showroom

SÉ ENSEMBLE Showroom

FROM CONCEPT STORE TO LIFESTYLE RETAIL: THE EMERGENCE OF MULTIFUNCTIONAL SPACES

KATHARINA MICHALSKI—Trend Researcher, Founder of Culture Dots

In markets characterized by complexity and abundance, the role of physical retail is in flux. Retailers increasingly transcend sectors and categories to curate an experience through the lens of an aspirational lifestyle.

When Colette, the iconic Parisian store, announced its closure at the end of 2017, the news created a stir among the fashion and design community. For 20 years, the avant-garde concept store was known to constantly redefine the shopping experience. Colette was not exactly a department store, even though its range spanned numerous categories from clothes and skincare to magazines and gadgets. Instead of wanting to be exhaustive, Colette scouted the world for high-quality products that were fresh and idiosyncratic. And rather than stocking entire collections, Colette distilled the few key pieces that reflected its ethos. Besides a considered selection, the concept store became synonymous with skillful juxtaposition that created surprise. Luxury labels were contrasted with streetwear brands, and established designers sat alongside newcomers. Most renowned, however, was Colette for its buzzworthy collaborations, which brought together unlikely partners and which cumulated in exclusive and highly coveted product designs. Constant variety and novelty were important to the retailer, who wanted to disrupt people's routines and reinforce a sense of discovery. All in all, Colette was not simply a store; it served as a platform for everything cool in pop culture. So when a store so adept at capturing the zeitgeist decided to call it quits, it may well be an indication that something else was nearing its end too.

Founded by a mother and daughter duo in an effort to demolish the boundaries separating style, music, art, and food, Colette represented the new wave of concept stores that were springing up all over the world in the 1990s and 2000s. They include 10 Corso Como, which opened in Milan in 1990; Opening Ceremony, created in New York in 2002; and Dover Street Market, founded in London in 2003. Taking inspiration from art galleries, concept stores impart value by using markers of curation, such as precisely mapped out and arranged objects, impeccable selection, vitrines, and descriptions on the wall. This curatorial approach frames the experience and creates context for the brands and products on display. What's more, all items are carefully selected across categories while adhering to a unifying creative vision informed by a sense of style, discerning taste, or unparalleled expertise. Successful concept stores are run by people who can pick what's cool and trending in the world or have a trained eye for the best of the best. Proliferation of these stores was driven by the recognition that the value of retail lies in curating merchandise and not in stocking and shifting. And with e-commerce on the rise, discovery over supply has become the stronghold of physical retail.

The transformation of retail

This transformation within physical retail started about 30 years ago and was driven by an unprecedented level of productivity that replaced scarcity with abundance. As a consequence, excess choice became a daily feature of our lives. The overload started with consumer goods, but it is now prevalent in all areas of life. While having options is a good thing, the problem we are now facing is a "tyranny of choice," a condition where too much choice creates anxiety or a state of being overwhelmed. In a world characterized by oversupply and complexity, brands and retailers play a significant role as filter mechanisms. Brands can simplify choice by signaling quality or other relevant values. Retailers can present us with a careful preselection that leaves us with better choice. In this context, the role of a retailer is increasingly that of a curator. As Michael Bhaskar, the author of *Curation: The Power of Selection in a World of Excess,* put it, "what's changing is not that retailers are curating, for at some level they have always done so; it's the focus on curation as retailers' raison d'être." This doesn't just apply to high-involvement products like fashion, but increasingly to all sectors. The supermarket chain Wholefoods, for instance, curates its stock by selecting products that represent ethical values and cater to a healthy lifestyle. The bookshop Waterstones helps customers discover interesting reads by selecting merchandise based on their local staff's personal recommendations. Retail curation is everywhere, but its nature is changing.

While the 1990s and 2000s were all about channeling pop culture, the 2010s are about signaling a lifestyle. The underlying principle, however, is the same: to create something new by rearranging elements from across different categories and sectors. The results are multifunctional spaces that cannot be easily categorized. While Colette was one of the first retailers to combine a store, a gallery, and a restaurant,

In today's world characterized by oversupply and complexity, brands and retailers play a significant role as filter mechanisms.

its co-founder Sarah Andelman concedes that, "with everything that already exists out there, it's really hard to do something new." It seems that the closure of Colette also marks the beginning of a new era in which the three-dimensional space is used for immersive storytelling, with the aim of navigating complex and saturated markets through the lens of a lifestyle.

Lifestyle retail on the rise

Take The New Road Residence as an example. The luxury guesthouse was created by the London-based fashion store Hostem based on the notion of a "curated residence," where guests can buy some of the furniture and home accessories at the end of their stay. As Hostem's artistic director explains, "Hostem has an opinion on ceramics and lifestyle but isn't necessarily the outlet for it." Their vision found expression in the contextual hospitality space infused with highly personalized and experiential shopping elements, allowing guests to immerse themselves in a lifestyle centered on pared-down luxury, exclusivity, and tranquility. By the same token, the Ace Hotel group pioneered a hospitality concept built around a creative lifestyle that promotes communal values. From its very beginnings, Ace Hotel aspired to be the extension of people's living rooms; every Ace Hotel branch becomes unique by instilling the identity of the respective location into its brand. Before opening in east London in 2013, for example, the designers explored the area to understand what made it distinct. The goal was to blend in and enrich the lives of the local community. The result is a space that enables interplay between hospitality, retail, entertainment, leisure, and work and that is renowned for its event programming and brand collaborations, for example with tokyobike or A.P.C. Its publicly accessible space houses a florist, a cold-pressed juice bar, a record store, the restaurant Hoi Polloi, and a gym with a climbing wall. The heart of Ace Hotel London, however, is the communal lobby-cum-co-working space frequented by local freelancers and entrepreneurs. The hotel mirrors the vibrant and creative lifestyle of east London, which attracts a certain crowd to whose aspirations and values it appeals.

Berlin- and London-based The Store, which has a loose partnership with the Soho House group, represents the evolution of the concept store on a mission to "redefine luxury." The Store blurs the boundaries between art, culture, lifestyle, and fashion, and offers "a new kind of retail, creative, and social experience." Each space has a different focus: in London, The Store emphasizes creative collaboration and houses studios and creative workspaces, whereas in Berlin it offers a curated retail experience of fashion, furniture, music, art, and books. In addition, exhibitions and collaborations with artists, fashion designers, craftsmen, and chefs are integral to The Store. Last year, for example, The Store housed a critically acclaimed exhibition in collaboration with the Hayward Gallery in London. This year, it was home to the creative partnership between Louis Vuitton and Supreme. Creative director Alex Eagle describes The Store as an "open, shopable private home for everyone to spend time, and where everything is for sale from the candle burning and the record playing to the sofa you sit on." In other words, The Store offers a total experience that welcomes people to spend all day in the retail space.

While retailers like The Store have long borrowed from the arts, cultural institutions have only recently begun to embrace consumerist culture to court their audiences. The arts writer and editor David Balzer observed that exhibitions were beginning to "behave like high-end fashion shows, generating desirability for specific works, and (…) asserting trends." Now, according to art historian and curator Kimberly Chrisman-Campbell, the lines are even more blurred, with blockbuster fashion exhibitions starting to function as high-end boutiques. For instance, Alexander McQueen: Savage Beauty at New York's Museum of Modern Art in 2011 and The Fashion World of Jean Paul Gaultier at the Montreal Museum of Fine Arts were selling limited-edition fashion pieces that were not available anywhere else. As Balzer explains, "The cultural institution wants, like participatory art, a lack of a finite relationship with its audience." The objective is to increase dwell time and deepen engagement with the institution's brand, as well as keep people interested in coming to and being in those spaces.

Focus on brand coherence and usefulness

Companies increasingly approach their physical space in a similar way. The women's activewear brand Sweaty Betty opened a flagship store that includes a café, a blow-dry bar, and a fitness studio—its first permanent experiential retail space. The store offers a complete fitness, food, and beauty package that captures the essence of the brand: "To inspire women to find empowerment through fitness." The brand only collaborates with carefully selected partners that reflect the lifestyle with which it wants to be associated. As a result, visitors can participate in classes led by boutique fitness studios GymClass and Frame, eat healthy dishes served by the vegan café Farm Girl, and book a blow-dry from Duck & Dry. The challenge in lifestyle retail is to ensure a selection is coherent with the brand by creating something aspirational.

The paradox of lifestyle retail is that by adding elements, complexity is cut down. In an overloaded world, brands like Sweaty Betty examine what's already available and recombine the elements in a meaningful way. How things are arranged and framed changes how we view them, and therefore influences our attitudes and actions. The focus on convergence creates new categories that help make sense of the world. The New Road Residence and Ace Hotel are not just defined by their function (offering a place to sleep), but by the idiosyncratic ways of life they encourage. By the same logic, The Store is not just a high-end boutique; it's a platform to explore the complex relationship between luxury and creativity.

But the most important thing is to be useful. As Michael Bhaskar put it, "When [retail] curation is built around a sense of what others want, imbued with service ethic—when it cares about what it curates more than the curation itself—curation becomes highly valuable." Lifestyle retail is not just about add-ons like cafés and communal tables; it's about bringing elements together to create something that is more than the sum of its parts. At its most useful, lifestyle retail makes the most of what's already available and distills what matters. And in doing so, retailers can help consumers make better choices. <

GENTLE MONSTER

Gentle Monster's spectacular stores make us take off the prescription frames and rub our eyes in amazement. Imbued with surreal stories and curious ideas, the Korean eyewear brand's whimsical retail concepts remind us that it is not merely OK to be odd, it may possibly even pay off.

"Nobody wants to see the normal, the contemporary customer craves the captivating," explains Jae Ho Bae, Gentle Monster's head of retail design. Unwearyingly working toward the unexpected, he and his team develop immersive interiors that surpass Gentle Monster's peculiar products in strangeness and media impact—and have thus tremendously contributed to the brand's recent success. "We love to be weird," says Mr. Bae. "If you will, weirdness is Gentle Monster's main strength." It was not initially meant to be.

When entrepreneur Hankook Kim founded Gentle Monster back in 2011, he reputedly first sought to establish an eyewear company à la Warby Parker; one that would combine a classic, yet contemporary style with reasonable prices. But facing the fashion industry's erratic interests and an ever-growing array of sleek spectacle stores, Mr. Kim carved out a pleasantly different path. Having gained first international fame through glossy celebrity placements, >

The New Generation, After Tsunami, Chengdu Store

The New Generation, After Tsunami themed flagship in Chengdu, China, represents a post-tsunami world in which the customer's shopping experience is enhanced via an eclectic range of elements, decorations, and materials. The store's two levels are connected by a giant swirling staircase—the tsunami. Everything on the ground floor is captured in dramatically illuminated black and gray hues. Moving sculptures suspended from the ceiling symbolize reemerging life forms and the resilience of nature.

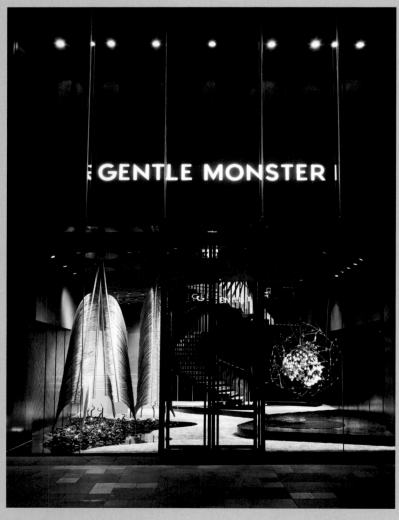

One floor up at *The New Generation*, the color palette shifts from dark hues to light. The space feels airy and less oppressive. This is a nascent world in which tube-like fibers sprout from a perforated steel wall and fragile plant-like forms dance in the light. You almost need to search for the merchandise in this surreal landscape. Arranged discreetly on the shelving or custom-built displays, it blends seamlessly into the interior.

Driven by flights of wild imagination, Gentle Monster's retail concepts draw inspiration from just about anything, including natural disasters and Nietzsche.

he began to expand on the distinctive K-Pop twist of his brand and soon caused a furor with store designs that—much like the heavily synthesized, all-encompassing pop culture genre—exhibit an extremely wide spectrum of influences and ideas.

Driven by flights of wild imagination, Gentle Monster's retail concepts draw inspiration from just about anything, including natural disasters and Nietzsche. The brand's flagship in Chengdu, China, for example, imagines a world washed away by a tsunami. But instead of painting a barren, post-apocalyptic picture, it translates the serious worldly threat into a surreal landscape richly repopulated by fresh forms of life. Similarly dreamy in the attempt to transfer a serious topic into a fabulous mise-en-scène, Gentle Monster's Singapore store takes its >

"Nobody wants to see the normal, the contemporary customer craves the captivating."—Jae Ho Bae, Head of Retail Design, Gentle Monster

cues from of the circle life in *Thus Spoke Zarathustra*, depicting its three metamorphoses—camel, lion, and child—as a series of enchanting installations. Like large philosophical disquisitions, the weird-looking creatures leave us searching for both meaning and eyewear frames amidst the artful installations—and the missing link between them both.

That said, the product per se proposes itself as a symbol of discovery—a theme that runs through Gentle Monster's work as a virtually invisible thread. Picking it up in Daegu, Korea, one finds the fictional hideout and secret laboratory of David Sakhai, "a supplier of pigments and materials for forgery," who appears to be inspired by the eponymous American art dealer and counterfeiter Ely Sakhai. But instead of canvases, paints, and brushes, the store's interior is fitted with clotheslines and rows of washing machines. Is Ely Sakhai's Asian namesake a forger of fashion, specialized in the recoloring of clothes? Mr. Bae, the retail design director, is careful to not >

Frogism, Shanghai Store

Curious mechanized structures are at play at *Frogism*, the brand's store in the IFC Mall in Shanghai's financial district. The name merges "frog" and "sadism," and the concept finds inspiration in a phrase from George Orwell's allegorical novel *Animal Farm*. On entering the store, the customer is drawn to these sculptural machines, while the brand's coveted sunglasses and prescription eyewear are subtly presented on sleek, wall-mounted shelves in the background.

The Platform, Hong Kong Flagship Store

Gentle Monster's Hong Kong flagship store, *The Platform*, illustrates the story of this bustling city, a place at the heart of Asia, in which diverse cultures coexist. In a series of "sets" that are reminiscent of stills from a Wes Anderson movie, the scheme conjures up the atmosphere of a train station, with tiled walls, sliding doors, and bench seating. One area mimics the inside of a passenger car, in which the merchandise is arranged on a shelved window-like display. Another gives the impression of a passing train, with a row of mirrors for windows.

Restoring the sense of mystery that much of modern life tends to lack, the displays ask the consumer to explore, connect the dots, and, eventually, discover hidden connections.

The Artisan,
Shanghai Flagship Store

At *The Artisan*, the brand's flagship store in Shanghai, China, the theme is craftsmanship, with an emphasis on the various steps of production from raw materials to finished product. The striking window displays on the street side show different stages of construction. One details the process of transforming a felled tree into lumber; the next houses an abstract sculpture within a timber framework.

reveal much, so the idea remains shrouded in mystery, like many of Gentle Monster's designs. Restoring the sense of mystery that much of modern life tends to lack, they ask the consumer to explore, connect the dots, and, eventually, discover hidden connections.

Tied together by the common ambition to take the customer on an adventurous journey, Gentle Monster's retail concepts are often linked to their respective locations. In Hong Kong, a vintage-inspired interior resembling the artful sets of Wes Anderson's movies references the city's image as a vibrant intercultural hub using a candy-colored train theme. In Shanghai, a city where technological progress, ancient arts, and cyberpunk culture collide, Mr. Bae and his team recreated an artisan's wood workshop, contrasting organic materials such as sawdust and tree trunks with metal sculptures and monotonous, industrial soundscapes. Back in Korea, their store in Seoul's traditional Bukchon Hanok Village aims to >

raise the customer's awareness for "all the good old things that tend to be forgotten." Housed in a historic bathhouse, it combines ancient architectural features with sleek white shelves.

Sleekness is generally none of Gentle Monster's business. An exception may be the brand's first flagship outside of Asia, which opened in NYC's SoHo district in 2016. According to Mr. Bae, the reason for it being surprisingly minimalistic is not a matter of different customer expectations but simply the result of a different creative handwriting: the store was designed by Rafael de Cárdenas of Architecture at Large, whose graphic visual language appears remarkably subtle compared to Gentle Monster's. "We love to collaborate and work with artists, furniture brands and designers," Bae explains. "But in general, all our retail concepts are developed in-house, which is maybe the reason for this one going a bit out of line. Gentle Monster's products are great, but the >

Secret Laundry, Daegu Store

In Daegu, South Korea, *Secret Laundry* creates a focal point with a bank of launderette-style washing machines, alongside an installation featuring wire shopping carts laden with compact cubes of compressed linens. The merchandise is displayed on brightly lit shelves against a backdrop of lush palms. Customers can admire the latest styles in this surreal setting as they gaze at themselves reflected in large round mirrors suspended from the ceiling.

GENTLE MONSTER *Secret Laundry,* Daegu Store

Tied together by the common ambition to take the customer on an adventurous journey, Gentle Monster's retail concepts are often linked to their respective locations.

The Secret Appartment, Bejing Store

Taking surreal to another level, *The Secret Apartment* concept store in Bejing, China, centers on a series of rooms with a domestic theme. But the contents of each room are confused, as if each contains a riddle that must be solved. In the kitchen, for example, glasses are displayed on a series of turntables that run the length of the countertop. The office-cum-studio features multiple versions of Vermeer's *Girl with a Pearl Earring*. In the living room, a collection of ferns and palms all but consumes the fireplace. As customers pass from one space to the next, they find themselves on a journey of discovery that will certainly add up to a memorable experience.

Measured by Gentle Monster's standards, an effective store design is one that combines strangeness with beauty, which, according to Mr. Bae, are two sides of the same coin.

Embark,
Seoul Flagship Store

Gentle Monster's first flagship store, *Embark,* was opened in Seoul, South Korea. Arranged on two floors, the store's interior design comprises a sequence of small rooms, each with a different theme. As customers tour the store, they experience a range of moods that are cultivated through the use of color and ornament. As the brand's first store, one can only imagine how unique it must have seemed at the time it launched, a lasting journey at once disorientating and fascinating.

conceptual part is our specialty and something that we want to continue building upon."

Over the past years, Gentle Monster's creative department has grown to 80 employees in the fields of branding, marketing, product, and retail design. But hierarchies remain flat at the brand's headquarters in Seoul. Mr. Bae also emphasizes the importance of creative exchange: "We have a lot of brainstorming sessions, where everyone is invited to bring in suggestions. Basically, everything can serve as a starting point and be developed into an effective store design."

Measured by Gentle Monster's standards, an effective store design is one that combines strangeness with beauty, which, according to Mr. Bae, are two sides of the same coin. It relates back to their brand name, he says, which refers to an ambiguity deeply embedded in all human minds: "We all have a soft and sensitive side, but then again, there is always some sort of monster slumbering inside." Poised between the gentle and the grotesque, the brand's diverse retail concepts present themselves as perfectly >

Samsara, Singapore Store

Samsara in Singapore offers a multisensory sequence of scenes that take inspiration from Ron Fricke's visually stunning, non-narrative documentary *Samsara* (2011) and Friedrich Nietzsche's book *Thus Spoke Zarathustra* (1891). Abstract art installations provide interest and are accompanied by both sound and smell. The theme centers on the inescapable cycle of life and culminates in a giant infinity symbol, which drives the message home.

Poised between the gentle and the grotesque, the brand's diverse retail concepts present themselves as perfectly instagram-worthy and, perhaps most importantly, as ever-new.

instagram-worthy, and perhaps most importantly, as ever-new and explorable. It is, again, a matter of discovery, of finding beauty in the unorthodox materials Mr. Bae and his team employ so unsparingly—within stores, but especially in the prolific project spaces that Gentle Monster maintains as a creative testing ground.

Having occupied the first floor of their three-story showroom in Seoul's Hongdae neighborhood for almost two and a half years, the so-called Quantum Project probably best reflects the brand's unquenchable urge for renewal: reimagined every 25 days in collaboration with an extensive range of artists and brands, it has, among many other things, taken the form of the experimental bakery Flying Jam, a colorful ping-pong court, a greenhouse, and the egg-crate-clad "Daydream Oasis," complete with a pool of shimmering fabrics and foils. Since the series of pop-up installations ceased in late 2016, Gentle Monster's "extracurricular" creative ambitions have >

continued at the BAT project space. First launched as a café with a rooftop cornfield, it recently reopened as an immersive comic shop, and it is sure the temporary home of a diverse host of projects to come.

It is interesting to see Gentle Monster's curatorial approach feed into its flagships: the one in NYC includes an in-store art gallery to host rotating exhibitions against its otherwise understated backdrop—a good way to stay flexible for a creative department that doesn't like to busy itself with long-term strategies but operates impulsively in the present. "Sometimes we change the whole concept of a store within a week before the opening," Mr. Bae shares. "Today, we talked about a circus theme, a farm, and alternative energies, but all that may be nixed tomorrow. We are fast and fickle. Which is also why we always like our latest store best."

Having recently opened a second overseas store in LA, Gentle Monster intends to take over Europe in 2018. As Mr. Bae reveals, an appropriate London location has already been found. "Nothing is fixed yet, but within a few years, we will certainly be in Paris and other big cities, too. Eventually, the goal is to become the number-one brand in our sector." So consumers the world over can look forward to seeing the weird gain ground. <

Home and Recovery, Seoul Store

In the Sinsa district of Seoul, South Korea, *Home and Recovery* conjures up a space that blurs the lines between the domestic environment and one of recovery. Presented in a limited color palette in which white, gray, and blue dominate, this somewhat sterile showcase still exudes luxury. A vast, tiled bathroom sees merchandise displayed on fine marble shelving. In the bedroom, the same marble is cut into geometric slabs laid out on hospital-style beds, on which the brand's wares are displayed.

YANGZHOU Bookstore

For the Zhongshuge bookstore in the ancient river-side city of Yangzhou, China, XL-MUSE Architects drew inspiration from the city itself, using bridge and river motifs to feed the imagination.

Stepping into Yangzhou's Zhongshuge bookstore is like entering one of the futuristic worlds you might expect to encounter inside the pages of the books that line its shelves. Taking inspiration from the cityscape that surrounds the store, XL-MUSE Architects created a series of truly visionary spaces that make prolific use of the river motif. A tunnel of books leads from the entrance to the main hall, as if passing through the arch beneath a bridge, and a black glass floor creates water-like reflections. The arch motif is repeated in the softly lit reading room with its sinuous architectural details. From there, step into the bright lights of the reading forest where columns of books tower up to the mirrored ceiling and seemingly beyond. In the picture book pavilion, a space dedicated to children, the brightly colored furniture recreates the Yangzhou cityscape and features movable, interchangeable pieces that offer an interactive experience. In the children's room, as in all of the other spaces of the bookstore, visitors are encouraged to stretch their minds and let the imagination flow. <

A forest of mirrors wends its way across the front window of the store. Nestled within the mirrored "trunks," narrow shelves lined with books reach all the way from floor to ceiling.

GNOMO Concept Store

MASQUESPACIO's design for Gnomo's new concept store combines a 1980s design aesthetic with contemporary display elements. Numerous arrangements can be used to present objects from a wide set of brands without creating visual disorder.

From the get-go, Gnomo is as cheery, whimsical, and fun as its namesake (*gnomo* is Spanish for "gnome"). Even when the store is closed, its façade giving no clue as to what lies within, the curvaceous lettering and candy-colored stripes are friendly and inviting. Raise the shutters, and the store reveals a haven for lovers of quirky design wares. A concept store promoting a wide range of brands, Gnomo celebrated its sixth birthday with a move to the hip Ruzafa district of Valencia, Spain. The awarding-winning creatives behind Masquespacio are responsible for its current incarnation, creating a uniform look that identifies Gnomo without detracting from the goods on sale. They pull it off by combining black, grid-like tables and wall panels with quirky pastel-colored display stands that can be arranged in an infinite number of configurations. There is an air of 1980s postmodernism here—a minimalism and geometry that hark back to the Memphis days in flat colors, allowing the products to shine. <

GNOMO Concept Store

KINDO Kids' Boutique

ANAGRAMA's creation for trendy kids' clothing boutique Kindo consists of a huge model of a child's toy, providing a whimsical display of the brand's wares in colors that pop against a pure white background.

Kindo is a kids' clothing and accessories boutique situated in San Pedro Garza García, Mexico. Keen to promote itself as a brand that imbues classic design with a contemporary edge, the store commissioned Anagrama design studio to create the perfect environment for its wares. The design team centered the store's look on a giant bead maze, the threads of which weave their way around the store, strung here and there with huge geometric shapes. It is a playful design that appeals to children and adults alike, but it is also practical; the threads double as a hanging rail and the beads offer shelving on which to arrange accessories. In order to capture the brand's classic/contemporary vibe, Anagrama introduced one or two bright neon shades to an otherwise pastel color scheme and painted the rest of the room—floors, ceiling, and walls—a brilliant white. <

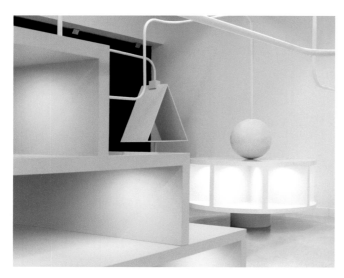

PETITE POMME Shop

Home-grown design firm ERBALUNGA ESTUDIO creates a whimsical playhouse interior for Tui-based Petite Pomme, purveyors of quality children's clothing. Bold color schemes and innovative displays attract the attention of parents and children alike.

Based in the small Spanish town of Tui in Galicia, Petite Pomme is an independent boutique selling high-end children's clothing and shoes. At the entrance, in striking juxtaposition to the store's historic granite exterior, a backlit polycarbonate wall lures customers into a contemporary, open-plan space dominated by playhouse structures reminiscent of kids' construction sets. An impressive ceiling allows for an interplay of scale and color. The interior is the work of local design firm Erbalunga Estudio and makes use of natural wood elements and scenographic lighting set off against huge expanses of primary colors. The structures within are fun to look at, but also direct you to the goods on display—a run of shoes is embedded in the backlit wall, a timber-frame house guides you along a rack of clothing. Displays are typically low so that children get a view, too. Best of all are the innovative displays that appeal to the kids who visit the store—a colorfully interactive wall of wooden slats and a giant pegboard from which to hang the finest of designer outfits. <

The team at Erbalunga Estudio had the good fortune of working within an original building of generous proportions. The false ceiling was removed to create the space which stages the playschool scheme.

BRAND UTILITY—TURNING BRAND PROMISE INTO A SERVICE

KATHARINA MICHALSKI—Trend Researcher, Founder of Culture Dots

When brands struggle to connect with their online audiences, physical retail must go beyond transaction and toward relationship-building between brand and customer. Guided by long-term thinking, brands create product-related services in exchange for trust and loyalty.

In 2014, Apple CEO Tim Cook famously announced, "You are not the customer; you are the product." He was taking direct aim at platforms like Google and Facebook, whose business model is to offer free online services in exchange for their users' privacy. There is a good reason for Apple to create distance from the business of data harvesting. Research released by the consultancy Prophet revealed that although people find Facebook and Google useful, when it comes to faith and confidence in handling their personal information, they simply don't trust these brands. As a result, Facebook barely makes the top 100 most relevant brands in Prophet's ranking, while Apple comes in at number one. Cook's attack on the advertising-powered platforms was accompanied by a pledge to protect Apple users' privacy. Instead of going after their data, Apple would pledge their trustworthiness first. Shortly after Cook's statement, the tech giant quietly introduced an ad-blocker to the mobile version of Safari—certainly to prove a point, but also to protect its sleek mobile devices from delivering a poor experience to their users. The more significant news, however, was Apple's biggest store redesign in 15 years. It marked a new take on physical retail as the main arena for building lifelong relationships between brands and customers.

Borrowing from the language of urban planning, Apple refers to its new stores as "town squares," indicating the tech giant's ambition to become an integral part of the cityscape. Apple's retail setup is organized into avenues, plazas, forums, and groves, inviting customers to dwell in the store as if it was an extension of their everyday urban experience. At the heart of the redesign is "Today at Apple," a program of free hands-on sessions intended to educate and inspire Apple's existing and future customers. Participants can learn photography or coding skills, and classes are offered at all skill levels from amateur to professional. What's remarkable about Apple's new service is its inclusivity: it caters to all segments, from young to old, and from home to professional user. The idea is not only to draw "everyone and anyone" into the store, but also to play a bigger role in people's lives. "We want people to say, 'Hey meet me at Apple,'" says Angela Ahrendts, Apple's SVP of retail.

When it comes to measuring success, two metrics matter to Ahrendts: how many people come to the store and how long they stay. After all, if you want to gain people's trust, you need to have their attention first. In order to make people gravitate toward its stores, Apple had to offer something relevant and valuable, something beyond the allure of its products. Based on the scarcity principle, which states that people value things more highly when they perceive them to be scarce, Apple identified

The notion of a helpful brand emerged about a decade ago, inspired by the software industry and its premise of inherent usefulness. "Brand utility" was extolled as the answer to what was increasingly perceived as superficial advertising.

learning, inspiration, and human connection as relevant and desirable to its brand and audience, making these aspects the cornerstones of its retail experience. Equally important, the idea of a daily changing program was developed to create novelty as a way to sustain interest in the brand. This combination of desirability, relevance, and novelty holds particular impact. In times when knowledge quickly becomes obsolete and skills must be constantly updated, Apple reinforces the reliance on its brand. By being helpful and offering relevant services, Apple has managed to make itself indispensable to people's lives.

Academic research had long identified a strong relationship between trust and affective commitment. Put another way, without trust there is no brand loyalty.

The notion of a helpful brand emerged about a decade ago, inspired by the software industry and its premise of inherent usefulness. "Brand utility" was extolled as the answer to what was increasingly perceived as superficial advertising. Instead of just selling, brands were supposed to make life easier and be genuinely helpful, the new mantra went. Nike was one of the first lifestyle brands that was seen as selflessly helpful when it launched its Nike+ running community app. Other brands followed suit: banks developed ATM finders, and hotels tweeted personalized city recommendations to disoriented travelers. However, apart from a few exceptions, user engagement with brand utility was relatively low. Martin Weigel, head of planning at Wieden+Kennedy, argued that the reason for this lack of appeal was that people generally didn't engage with a brand as much as the brand owners would like to

think they did. What was more crucial to its demise was that many brands approached brand utility as yet another advertising campaign. Instead of being a continuous effort, it was seen as a temporary venture; and instead of offering real value for the user, it demanded attention and, more often than not, valuable storage space.

The hype around brand utility was helpful in exposing the dissonance between the marketing message and the actual product. Clearly, brands needed to walk the talk. Admen Alex Bogusky and John Winsor, in their bestselling Baked In: Creating Products and Businesses That Market Themselves, urged brands to build products with their message baked in. In their view, brands had to deliver on their promise if they wanted to forge strong re-

As Apple, Patagonia, and Nudie demonstrate, brand utility works best when it creates human contact. Although digital offers many consumer-centric benefits, real contact and empathetic communication play a crucial part in building relationships.

lationships with customers. The key was to ensure consistency between the marketing strategy and the product and thereby create an authentic brand story, which consumers would love and share with others. According to Bogusky and Winsor, the apparel brand Patagonia, with its lifetime guarantee (its claim: built with "Ironclad Guarantee"), exemplified this idea: its message of sustainability is an integral part of the product. But Patagonia does more than delivering on its promise—it lives its core values by serving its customers. The Worn Wear initiative, for example, helps Patagonia customers buy less and thereby reduce the amount of clothing that ends up in landfill. Customers can learn how to fix their clothes, trade in used garments at any Patagonia store for recycling, or buy second-hand gear at a discounted price. By turning its promise into substance and offering an in-store service, Patagonia is

fostering a deeper connection with the customer that goes beyond one sale.

Another brand that converts purpose into a service is Nudie Jeans. Just like Patagonia, Nudie encourages conscious buying and ownership; and, it takes brand utility to the next level. Only two years after its launch in 2011, Nudie opened its first Repair Shop in native Stockholm, where customers can have their denim fixed, free of charge. Nudie conducts the service in-store at sewing stations equipped with heavy-duty machines. The reason for offering the repair service is rooted in the brand's commitment to sustainability: although Nudie only uses organic cotton, the plant is still one of the most poisonous to grow. By giving a pair of Nudie Jeans the longest life possible, the brand helps to curb cotton production. At the same time, Nudie promotes a conscious lifestyle by telling their customers that what they love is worth preserving and caring for: "We [at Nudie] believe that you should wear in and repair your jeans in order to create your own individual jeans stories," says founder Maria Erixon. Because the repair service is an integral part of the brand philosophy, Nudie is constantly opening new Repair Shops, with 26 operating worldwide. Just like Patagonia, Nudie sees more value in face-to-face contact with customers than in traditional advertising.

Extending product lifecycle not only benefits the customer and the environment, but also reveals Nudie's long-term thinking as a company. In an interview with the Guardian, Nudie CEO Palle Stenberg explained, "It's not about how much we spend to make one unit. It's about how long you can make a single pair of jeans last. People sometimes say that we'd earn so much more if we didn't have this service … yes we could, but that's not the point. We think long term." In other words, relationships take time to build and Nudie is willing to invest. Offering a free service

that encourages a conscious lifestyle as a non-opportunistic act is a trust-building exercise that fosters commitment and advocacy. Although market surveys have not been conducted to see if customers are likely to stick with the brand, "judging by the positive feedback we get, it seems to be the case," says Stenberg.

Academic research had long identified a strong relationship between trust and affective commitment. Put another way, without trust there is no brand loyalty. Researchers at the University of Paris found that brands earn trust when they show integrity, i.e. are sincere with their customers and express an interest in them; have credibility, i.e. consistently deliver on their promise; and demonstrate benevolence, i.e. go out of their way to satisfy the needs of their customers. In other words, brand utility has to be relevant to consumers, aligned with the brand promise, and offered consistently and reliably in order to build relationships based on trust.

For brands focusing on building relationships with their customers, physical retail is the platform that will allow them to bring the brand promise to life.

As Apple, Patagonia, and Nudie demonstrate, brand utility works best when it creates human contact. Although digital offers many consumer-centric benefits, real contact and empathetic communication play a crucial part in building relationships. Watching your favorite jeans getting fixed; being inspired by someone's story; making a connection that transforms your life; and learning something from another person—all of these things create memorable experiences, which in return foster a deeper connection with the brand that enables them. Luxury brands,

Watching your favorite jeans getting fixed; being inspired by someone's story; making a connection that transforms your life; and learning something from another person—all of these things create memorable experiences, which in return foster a deeper connection with the brand that enables them.

for example, have long harnessed the power of personal touch, which is hardly transferrable to the digital space. They also recognize that personalized service is one of the strongest brand differentiators, and that the physical store plays a key role in representing the brand.

Hermès is a case in point. The luxury brand recently rolled out a subscription service, for which interested customers can only sign up in-store. Because subscription services are synonymous with convenience, they are typically sold online. Hermès, however, positions the service as a membership, where customers become part of an exclusive community. Called Tie Society, customers pay a monthly fee for regular delivery of a carefully curated silk tie selection. The membership comes with exclusive perks, such as free laundering, tie reshaping, and repairs. To reinforce a sense of belonging, members are also invited to exclusive events and product launches at the brand's flagship stores. Hermès's subscription service not only demonstrates the importance of brand utility in the luxury sector, but also the value of human connection in creating enduring customer relationships. But it's not just retailers that add product-related services to foster relationships; it's also service providers that explore the potential of physical retail as a community-building measure. The tech startup WeWork, for example, which since its launch in 2010 evolved from a co-working to a community driven company, revealed plans to expand into physical retail. Its latest initiative may include adding short-term leases for retail stores or incorporating stores into its co-working spaces as an amenity for its users. The retail push comes as WeWork

It's not just retailers that add product-related services to foster relationships; it's also service providers that explore the potential of physical retail as a community-building measure.

increasingly branches out into new business lines that help the company to fulfill its mission to foster human connections. One of its latest acquisitions is Meetup, a digital company that brings people together around common interests and encourages them to get off the Internet and meet in real-life. The acquisition makes a lot of sense for WeWork that can now fill its space after hours with Meetup gatherings and thereby tap into a new group of potential customers to whom its credo "work to make a life, not a living" will likely appeal. Paired with carefully curated shopping elements, these service offerings may encourage

WeWork members to spend valuable leisure time on the premises and bond with other members over common interests and shared lifestyles.

All this indicates that WeWork strives to join the rank of retail companies, which realize the enormous value that lies in being the facilitator of real-life communities.

Adam Neumann, WeWork's CEO and co-founder, attributes this development to the trend of urbanization, where "people from every walk of life are seeking spaces in big cities that allow for human connection." Neumann sees retail as part of that movement. As Apple and WeWork

The key is to ensure consistency between the marketing strategy and the product and thereby create an authentic brand story, which consumers would love and share with others.

in particular demonstrate, the future will be about gaining control of the physical space and utilizing it to build relationships with customers. In this context, the role of the physical store will undergo a transition from a mere transactional to a relational space. For brands focusing on building relationships with their customers, physical retail is the platform that will allow them to bring the brand promise to life. The ultimate goal is to earn trust and turn it into lifelong commitment. This requires a continuous effort to understand what really matters to the customer. Creating brand utility might not be a shortcut to exuberant growth rates, but in the long run it will be one of the most rewarding investments a brand can pursue. <

L'ÉCHOPPE Concept Store

Parisian firm CUT ARCHITECTURES devised a grocery store concept for the display of menswear accessories in Tokyo-based L'Échoppe, with wares stacked high on open shelving, in pullout drawers, and even on trolleys and stepladders.

The ethos behind the L'Échoppe consumer experience is that even the best-dressed man has a gap in his wardrobe, be it a hat, a bag, or a pair of shoes; so instead of offering complete outfits to the man about town, L'Échoppe focuses on those perfect finishing touches. When asked to create the right environment for such a venture, the design team at CUT architectures based its concept on a French épicerie—the local store you go to for that one ingredient needed to complete a favorite recipe. In CUT's interpretation of the form, the entire ground floor, including the window display, is equipped with floor-to-ceiling Vitsoe 606 shelving, designed by Dieter Rams in 1960. As soon as a customer walks into the store, he is able to see the wide range of goods on offer, including accessories, clothing, and cosmetics. Épicerie motifs feature elsewhere, from the canvas awnings of the second-floor decor to a range of trolley-style furnishings and beautifully tiled floors throughout. <

THE PARK.ING GINZA Concept Store

Commissioned to design the interior of The Parking.ing Ginza, a trendy clothing and lifestyle concept store housed in an underground parking garage, Japanese design firm NOBUO ARAKI/THE ARCHETYPE allowed the existing structure to dictate both style and substance.

The Parking.ing Ginza concept store, which occupied the third and fourth basement levels of Tokyo's Sony Building, was so in tune with its environment that it was not always easy to discern where the store ended and the parking garage began. Consisting of a café, retail space, and gallery, the store's various components were dispersed around the garage, wedged between parking spaces and the attendant's kiosk. Aimed at the young urban shopper, this unusual mix of elements was undeniably playful and cool. The store had no defining walls or even doors, just the odd strip of AstroTurf to designate different spaces. The intentionally temporary existence of the store was reflected in the materials used in its construction and display. Metal grid fencing and makeshift timber frameworks housed clothing on warehouse racks, while grooming products were displayed on shelves in alcoves between the parking spaces. The café displays an unexpected departure from style, with its whitewashed plaster walls and terra-cotta roof tiles evoking a rural hacienda. <

THE PARK.ING GINZA Concept Store

adidas—DAS 107 Concept Store

With the look of an industrial space such as a warehouse or a depot, URBANTAINER's design for the adidas concept store in Seoul effortlessly lures street-savvy, brand-conscious clientele through its doors.

DAS 107 is an adidas concept store located in the Hongdae district of Seoul, South Korea, an area known for its youthful urban vibe. This is where the street savvy hang out, making it the perfect location for showcasing top-of-the-line streetwear from adidas. Local studio Urbantainer's concept for the store's design is all about the street. Raw concrete walls, hardwearing ascon flooring, pebble trenches, and custom-made zinc furniture set the scene. Raised sidewalks lead customers along the racks of clothing and road markings that start outside the building and continue on the inside. This inside-outside design speaks to a youthful clientele in a language they understand: the language of the street. There is a robustness and informality that encourages young adults to hang out together, while checking out the latest must-have gear. <

<u>adidas</u> Pop-Up Shop

Pushing the boundaries of fashion production and retail, adidas invited customers to take the lead role in a new, interactive design concept. The 'Knit For You' pop-up shop was temporarily installed in Berlin's Mitte neighborhood and lured passersby with the promise of a bespoke merino sweater, co-created by them and knitted on the spot.

The scheme was realized in collaboration with Alexandra of Berlin-based creatives, The Bakery. The idea is that customers use the latest body-scanning technology to create a perfect-fit merino sweater in their chosen color that is then knitted on location. In order to entice the customer, and with some 200 ready-made sweaters at her disposal, Alexandra created "walls" of sweaters in all available colors and patterns, suspended simply on geometric structures hanging from a grid overhead, each sweater out-stretched in full glory. From a distance, the display almost has the look of an abstract mural, with the sweaters taking shape as you get nearer. It is at once intriguing and arresting. There is a deliberate minimalism at play here—the large, open floorspace remains uncluttered and neutral in color and, save for a few fully dressed mannequins, there is no other clothing on display—just the sweater in its many different patterns and colors. The concept is a clever one that allows customers to invest their own creativity in the making of the clothes that they wear, so guaranteeing satisfaction time and time again. <

adidas Pop-Up Shop, Berlin

COTTON REPUBLIC Flagship Store

With its design for Cotton Republic's shopping-mall-based store in Beijing, Chinese design studio RAMOPRIMO devised an innovative, color-intense shelving system that draws attention across the mall.

In 2017, Cotton Republic, purveyor of fun and funky underwear, opened its flagship store in a Beijing shopping mall. Faced with a tiny unit that was fully glazed on the only two sides exposed to passersby, the design studio Ramoprimo set about devising a shelving system that could display items inside and outside the store at the same time. The solution lay in the large, woven, basket-like structure that spirals up the window like a wraparound rollercoaster. Painted in a palette of neon colors, the resulting structure is certainly eye-catching and attracts the attention of potential customers. It also allows for plenty of shelving in a relatively small space. Items can be placed on the shelves in such a way that they are visible no matter which side of the glass one is standing on. Furthermore, the open-weave structure maintains a level of transparency where more conventional shelving systems would not, thus enhancing the customer's spatial and sensorial shopping experience. <

NIKE

You name it, Nike just does it: with interactive retail environments, pop-up events, in-store customization booths, and site-specific installations in the streets of the world's hippest neighborhoods, the American sport giant defends its leading position in innovative retail. As tough as these times may be for brick-and-mortar sales—to Nike, it's nothing but a challenge.

Nike Air Max Day 2016, Hong Kong

By Rosie Lee

*Right_*In order to make the low-rise venue stand out in its high-rise setting, the designer clad the building in primary-colored pipes, funnels, and exposed structures, making it visible from a distance (see next page).

*Below_*Nike also installed a revolving shoe display on the roof.

There were times when Michael Jordan's ability to succeed in pressure-packed playoffs was more famous than his iconic series of Nike sneakers. Notoriously brilliant at making the break in difficult situations, the former NBA star delivered when competing under the toughest circumstances. Nike-endorsed tennis pro Roger Federer considers the capability to "play with pain, play with problems, play in all sorts of conditions" a core strength. Lance Armstrong, too, was a famous fighter before his Nike deal and cycling career were shattered by the infamous doping scandal.

Tapping into the competitive spirit of its long-standing collaborators, Nike's retail strategy scores with agility and the readiness to thrive under >

This page_Inside the building, the designer set up the Nike Innovation Kitchen, deconstructing the brand's latest innovations.

Opposite_Elsewhere, a gallery-type display showcases the leading designs of the shoe's 30-year history.

pressure. Alongside the brand's permanent flagship stores, a plethora of Swoosh-labeled events and temporary brand spaces are popping up at record speed in international metropolises. "You look at the market and know that others are working hard as well to set the bar higher," says Mark Smith, Nike's Senior Creative Director of Innovation. Responsible for the "special projects" that keep bubbling out of the brand's industrious creative department, he and his team have made it their mission to reliably stand at the forefront of the marveling rest.

"The consumer today expects a premium experience, with innovative product and services delivered faster and more personally," says the company's chairman, president, and CEO, Mark Parker. In response to the need for speed brought on by the internet age, Nike is streamlining its supply chain. To bring the resulting flow of fresh products to the people, it has updated its retail business with projects that double down on innovation, speed, and direct consumer interactions. Dubbed the "Triple Double >

Nike collaborated with French streetwear brand Pigalle and design practice Ill-Studio to install a colorful basketball court in a gap between two buildings in Paris.

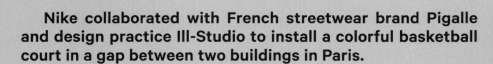

Strategy," the company's winning formula is perhaps most impressively reflected in its famous personalization and co-creation projects, like the Nike Makers' Experience that churns out custom shoes in less than 90 minutes. Installed in the brand's NYC-based Nike By You Studio, the live-design machine demonstrates Nike's ability to harness new technology to deepen its bond with consumers. "The intention of the project is to bring to life the collaborative design experience that we offer our athletes," says Smith, whose department headed the development of Nike's newest customization system. Like in sports, not everyone can be in the front row, so the installation is, at least initially, reserved for friends, family, and Nike+ members. While sports stars sign multimillion dollar endorsement deals, loyal Nike customers register online to benefit from the brand's manifold "special projects". >

Ill-Studio & NIKElab Pigalle basketball court, Paris

The Pigalle Duperré basketball court occupies an empty lot in the 9th arrondissement of Paris, its shape dictated by the somewhat irregular footprint. This project was a collaboration between Nike, the streetwear label Pigalle, and the creatives from Ill-Studio, who worked with gradients of blue, pink, purple, and orange to combine art and athletics in their design.

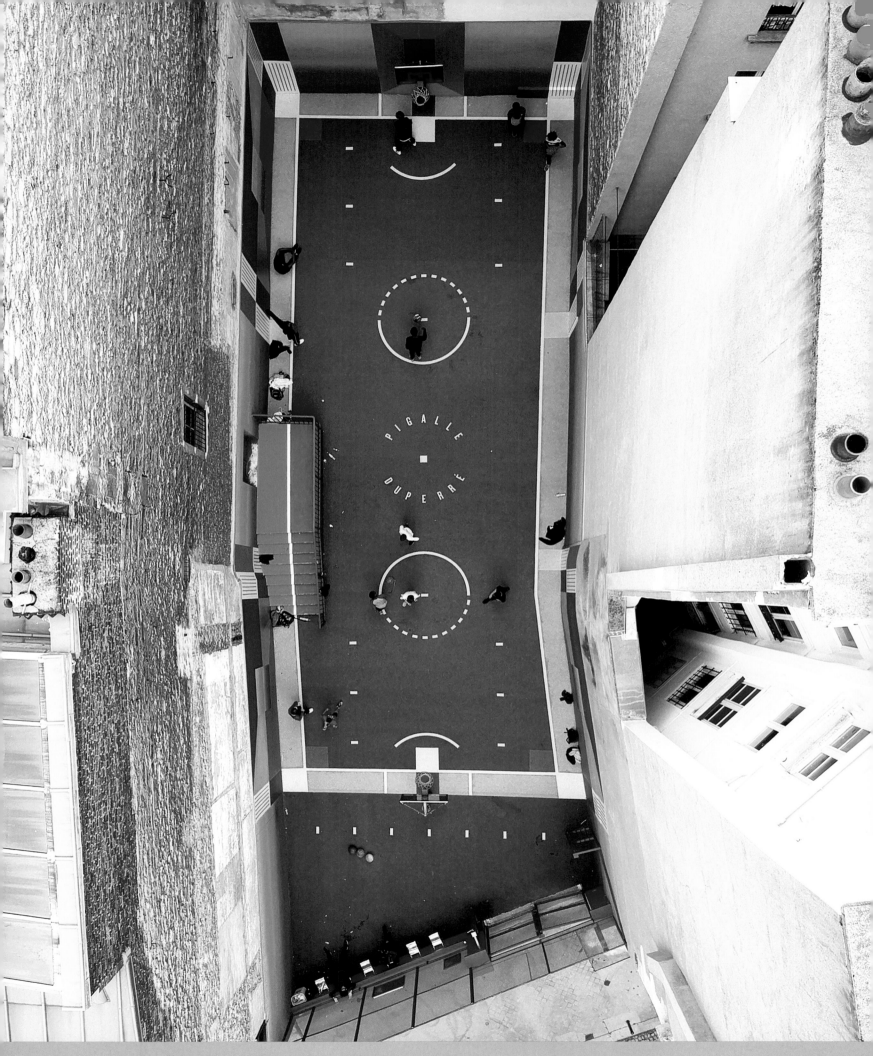

The seamless integration of digital tools allows Nike to identify shifting consumer tastes and render physical retail points "more personal, more mobile, more distinctive." As Parker told analysts, "The consumer has decided digital isn't just a part of the shopping experience, but the foundation of it." Pointing toward the increasing impact of these fast-changing appetites on consumer traffic and the overall economics of brick-and-mortar retail, Parker expects the near future of the physical store to be that of a promotionally driven environment. With Nike, he is heading a firm that has already turned this vision into a viable reality.

"No matter if it is the design you are working on or the tools you are using, be a visionary," says Tinker Hatfield, Nike's Vice President for Design and "special projects". Originally hired as the company's corporate architect in 1981, Hatfield spent his >

**Nike Opening
Finals 2017,
Portland**

By StoreyStudio

The design for *Nike Opening Finals 2017* has a raw, industrial vibe with its monochromatic palette and metallic finishes. A flanked entrance tunnel is lined with models of Nike shoes from past to present displayed on crumbling concrete pedestals.

> "No matter if it is the design you are working on or the tools you are using, be a visionary."—Tinker Hatfield, Vice President for Design & Special Projects, Nike

first four and a half years designing office spaces, showrooms, and stores. When he began designing shoes, they were often inspired by buildings. "If you want to create something special, look outside the playing field," Hatfield explains. For one of his first shoe designs, he looked to Centre Pompidou in Paris, especially at its exposed structures. The result was the Air Max, with its iconic window revealing the air cushioning in the heel. Thirty years later, the story of the architecture-inspired shoe has come full circle with an Air Max—influenced brand environment by Rosie Lee. Commissioned to develop an event-based initiative that would activate Nike's Air Max Day on the Chinese market for two consecutive years, the London-based creative studio designed two brand environments drawing on Hatfield's iconic inside-out concept. For the 2016 event, Hong Kong's famous Fringe Club was fitted with a rooftop installation featuring pipes, funnels, and exposed structures in primary colors. In 2017, Rosie Lee installed a super-sized crane machine game in the new venue's front windows, making part of the interior action >

Nike Air Max Day 2017, Shanghai

By Rosie Lee

Dubbed Air Land, the interior of a power station in Shanghai was transformed for *Air Max Day 2017* by Rosie Lee into a series of displays offering visitors an interactive journey through Air innovation. A series of vibrant, colorful, and interactive installations showcases key shoes from the Air Max line.

Although largely temporary—or exactly for this reason—Nike's "special projects" are memorable and have a lasting effect on the company's impeccable image.

Nike Sole DXB

By Rosie Lee

When Nike took part in Sole DXB in the UAE—a significant event for the latest designs in footwear, fashion, art, and design—Rosie Lee housed a contemporary showroom with plexiglass and neon displays inside an elevated shoe-box-shaped building, visible from miles around.

visible to passersby. Meanwhile, at Shanghai's 800 Show, customers were welcomed into Air Land, a bright environment inviting customers to interact with Air Max products. As part of the Remix My Airs project, artists were asked to create beats inspired by Air Max silhouettes. During the weekend, music acts and designers turned the space into a creative hub. As Hatfield put it, architecture is the "best example of the combination of art, science, and cultural experience." In Nike's brand environments, all three aspects come together to strengthen the brand's relationship with the broader cultural community.

Although largely temporary—or exactly for this reason—Nike's "special projects" are memorable and leave a lasting effect on the company's impeccable image. While the brand's flagship stores tend to be comparatively neutral to cater to the tastes of a broad target audience, its "special projects" sites stand out through striking visual concepts and attract a more

specific clientele. In 2014, Nike collaborated with French streetwear brand Pigalle and design practice Ill-Studio to install a colorful basketball court in a gap between two buildings in Paris. Enjoying popularity among local athletes and design fans alike, the project has recently been updated using a new, striking palette.

Another particularly eye-popping environment was created by the British set design studio of Robert Storey to present Nike Women's Fall Holiday Range 2014 at a NYC pop-up. To "evoke femininity in an urban context," Storey and his team defined a soft palette and set it against a sharply angular spatial structure. Inspired by the symmetry and sculptural installations of American minimalist Dan Flavin, the designers developed an hourglass-shaped space that immerses the audience in a narrative of iridescent lighting elements. Changing colors define individual stories and lead customers from collection to >

Nike GC CR7 Tour

By Rosie Lee

For an event celebrating footballer Cristiano Ronaldo's first-ever Chinese promotional trip, designers at Rosie Lee focused on the speed and explosiveness of Ronaldo's play. At the heart of their concept was a massive Nike Mercurial Superfly suspended from the ceiling—the player's signature shoe. It was constructed from over 1,000 rods of metal.

Inspired by the symmetry and sculptural installations of American minimalist Dan Flavin, the designers developed an hourglass-shaped space that immerses the audience in a narrative of iridescent lighting elements.

Nike FAHO 14 Pop-up

By StoreyStudio

Geometric forms and soft neon colors are the hallmark of StoreyStudio's design for this *Nike FAHO 14* pop-up shop. Clothes are displayed on rails that divide windows cut into thin walls, with each zone represented by a different color.

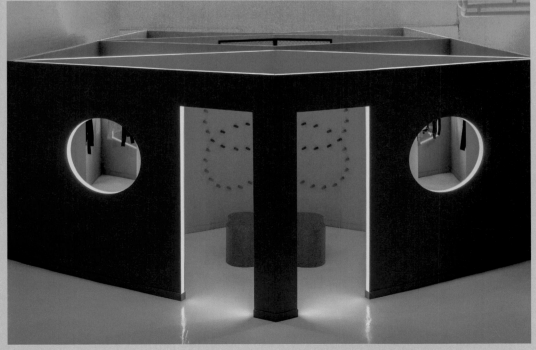

NIKE Nike FAHO 14 Pop-up

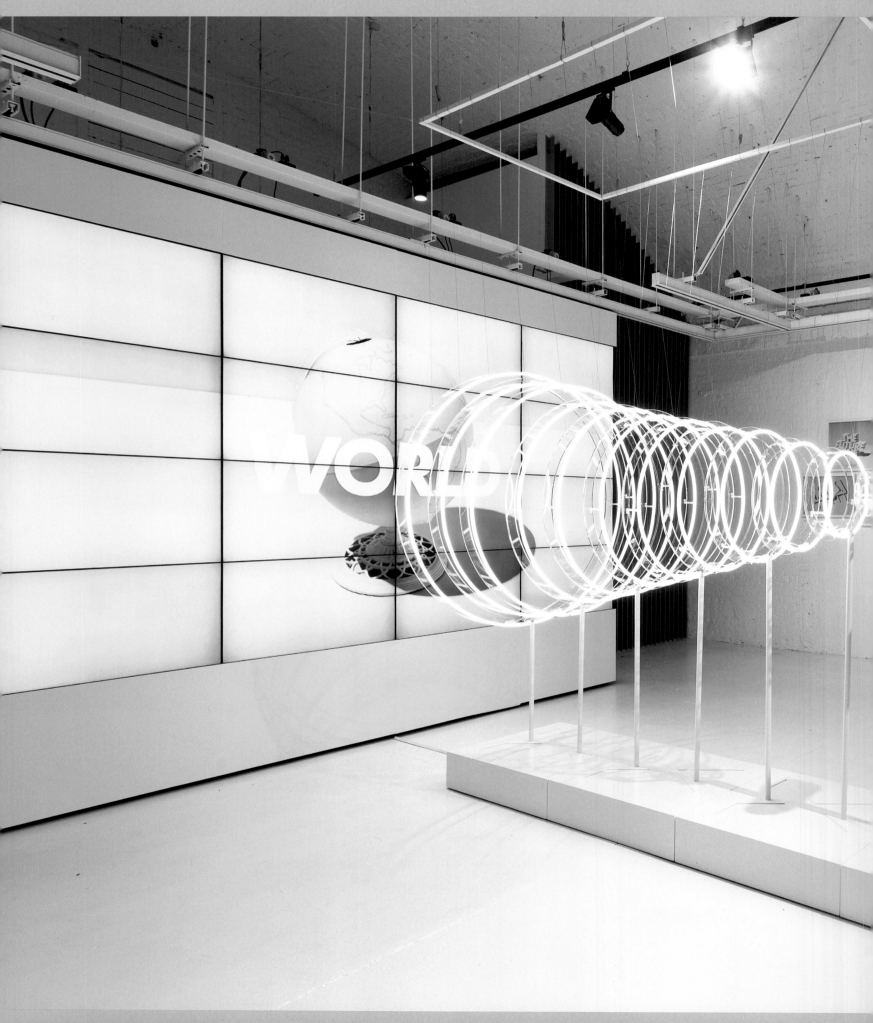

FROM AIR   TO LUNAR

In response to the need for speed brought on by the internet age, Nike is streamlining its supply chain.

Nike Lunar Force 1 Launch, London

By Rosie Lee

Rosie Lee developed an understated design to celebrate the 30th anniversary of Nike's Air Force 1 shoe that reflects the shoe's white color. The campaign cataloged the shoe's 30-year heritage, using a range of white and neon installations.

fitting room to NTC training space. The studio chose their visual means "in a playful and representational manner, always bringing the viewer back to the core purpose: sport." In a more recent project for Nike, StoreyStudio designed a space to host 166 young football players who qualified for the Opening Finals 2017 in Oregon. Located on Nike's Portland campus, the monochromatic result combines the purposeful simplicity of a locker room with a white-cube elegance. Exhibiting a selection of Nike cleats on illuminated concrete pedestals, a metal-clad tunnel provides entry into more functional zones like a players lounge, recovery area, and even a barber shop for the athletes.

Successful enough to swoosh away any doubts raised against large brick-and-mortar investments, the list of Nike's retail event spaces continues. As Chairman Parker notes, what we are seeing right now is "only a snapshot" compared to "the relentless flow of exceptional projects and platforms currently on the way." In the words of an old Nike slogan, "Runs end. Running doesn't."   <

THE RISE OF THE INNOVATION BOUTIQUE

KATIE BARON—Trends Forecaster & Head of Retail at Stylus.com

Now that innovation has become the byword for brand success—the golden ticket spawned by the ideals of start-up culture—the pursuit of spatial design has turned into a serious, ingenious, and extremely exciting business, fostering and housing cutting-edge activities. More culturally relevant than ever before, these stores boldly blur the boundaries between brands and their fans by creating experimental beta landscapes that represent a positive new blueprint for commercial culture.

The first type of this new breed of rule-evading brand spaces is the Expo Store (also known as Teaser Spaces). They satisfy the voracious desire for newness, whether in the "top-10" and "trending-now" lists across news channels and lifestyle websites or in capitalizing on Insider Intelligence so beloved by early adopters. In any case, these lab-like spaces are designed to project a sense of getting ahead of the mainstream consumer curve.

The inception of this trend traces back to opening industry-only trade shows to the public, a shift designed to monetize marketing spending and democratize retail, much in the way that bloggers once challenged traditional critics of creative culture. When German retailer Zalando purchased Berlin's seminal fashion expo Bread & Butter in 2016, aptly declaring the festival's theme NOW that year, it broke the circle of buyer-led exclusivity and empowered consumers to engage with brands on their own terms. Fusing retail, music, and entertainment, traditional booths became installations previewing items available for purchase online. The three-day event also included parties, panel talks, and stages for top acts.

While the inherently ephemeral nature of such retail has rendered some spaces the preserve of pop-up design, these spaces are increasingly taking more permanent shape. The B8ta store in California is a prime example. The sleek but inviting touch-feel-play-based showcase for hot tech goods feeds on FOMO (fear of missing out) by adding a regular influx of products, with no guarantee of how long they'll stick around. With lavish visual merchandising, Moscow store Trend Island honors its name by giving free retail space to new international talent for a 25 percent commission, ditching those that don't resonate just as quickly. And NYC-based # (Hashtag), a spin-off of US beauty brand Ricky's, stocks its shop floor with only Instagram-famous items or those recommended directly by customers in-store. Hence, the live hub is capable of both prompting and reflecting seductive social buzz.

Indeed, any brand with cutting-edge credentials or innovation in its midst can play the game. In a bid to show that it can keep up with the industry disruptors carving up its territory, Scottish bank Clydesdale designed Studio B Space in London as a cornucopia of fiscal reinvention. The glistening entrance resembles an urbane hotel lobby, while the interior is a movable, hybridized feast combining an interactive fintech expo, working innovation lab, and conventional bank branch. Tables are reconfigured into benches for industry meet-ups.

Sliding into the hospitality sector, the Scout bar in London has a private 10-seat lab in its basement. Here, visitors watch staff experiment with concoctions for future menus and get to taste the creations. American telecom brand Comcast created a Chicago flagship, Studio Xfinity, focused on "interaction, not transaction." This move illustrates the soft-sell character that accompanies the Expo Store trend. Its three theater-style studios host workshops, film screenings, product demos, and gaming nights, complemented by casual seating areas and a free bar. The space playfully contextualizes the company's most pressing product launches and the power of its intangible services. But the underlying message remains the same: get on board now or forever miss the boat.

HQ Hubs a. k. a. Gateway Spaces

Next comes the cousin of the Expo Store: the self-sharpening HQ Hub, or Gateway Space. It is also grounded in the desire for behind-the-scenes and insider access, but with the aim of boosting a consumer's personal sense of achievement. These concepts build traction by promising aspiring amateurs movement toward their professional goals or by simply closing the loop between fan culture and a company's internal practices.

Design tactics that present these stores as homes for career-boosting commerce are key. The concept is succinctly expressed in U. S. beauty brand Smashbox's London store, billed as the world's first Studio Store. Trading on its reputation as an industry insider's brand, the store design directly emulates its Los Angeles

In a time where transformation is key, innovation boutiques not only define a lucrative new world of fan-brand blended retailing but also prove their capacity to react to cultural seismic shifts at digital-era speed.

studio to convey professional relevance, reveling in professionally lit styling stations, free-wheeling test tables of products, and a bookable (but free) photographic studio and video booth. A triple whammy of transactional store, studio, and R&D platform, it shines a spotlight on the behaviors of its core audience in a way traditional focus groups cannot.

Similarly playing on the mutually beneficial practice of monetizing internal culture, British multi-brand skincare retailer Space NK's new London flagship hosts a space where customers are introduced to innovative products that have not been put on the market yet. The feedback from these exclusive product previews is then filed back to accelerate product development. Taking this idea into the communal setting, audio brand Sonos plugged into an opportunity for impromptu networking when it introduced its Sonos Studios global pop-ups. Audiophile consumers were partnered with record labels, event promoters, and musicians in co-working spaces and showrooms, diligently blurring the consumer/pro divide.

The specter of automation has catapulted this desire for self-optimization to new heights. In a world of searing competitiveness, amplified by the disbanding of traditional educational systems, it is never too early to cultivate professional smarts, especially if framed by a brand under the more playful guise of creative skills. Toy giant Lego's new Lego House flagship in Billund, Denmark, features expert-led creative labs where fans can submit product ideas. There's also a "social zone" for co-directing films (populated by Lego characters, naturally) and an area dedicated to stimulating visitors' cognitive abilities by engineering fictional cities and robots. The premise may be play but the peripheral extras for those who can afford a costly behind-the-scenes tour lasting two and a half days suggest there's considerably more learning to be had.

Topic Labs

In an era of increasingly activist attitudes, it is essential that brands are seen as taking a stance (political, social, and/or cultural). This has spurred the intrinsically innovation-wielding format of Topic Labs.

In an era of increasingly activist attitudes, it is essential that brands are seen as taking a stance—political, social, and/or cultural.

Driven by their very nature to keep moving, these are dynamic, spin-off spaces that align contemporary retail with cultural programming to transform stores into echo chambers of information gathered elsewhere. Retail here, as with all "innovation boutiques," is galvanized by its connections to the outside world.

Selfridges department store is an early pioneer of the strategy, repeatedly using its London flagship to demonstrate just how ardently it has its finger pressed to the social pulse. Store-wide programs have ranged from channeling innovation culture via its Festival of Imagination to promoting diversity through The Beauty Project, to rethinking identity, specifically via the lens of gender, with Agender. Newer to the table still, launching in 2018, U.S. denim label Hudson Jeans's LA flagship is going full "frenemy," aligning with competitors, if and when necessary, to generate change. Hosting other brands' events and projects rooted in art, performance, and design, the space will be grounded in emotionally charged topics, including youth and rebellion.

Finishing Salons

The marriage of product development and retail-rooted consumer engagement also offers innovation; this is visible in the world of Finishing Salons, spaces that contribute to the evolution of customization by interpreting consumer appetite for on-demand retail via an imaginative lens. While speed is imperative (semi-bespoke products can be created in hours, not months), spectacle is coming into play as well, countering the negative connotations of mindless convenience while keeping brand experience meaningful.

British online jewelry brand Vashi launched a new London flagship in November 2017 to offer an alternative to the traditional formality of diamond buying. Central to the retail experience is a creation process supported by craftspeople and gem specialists who are housed in a subterranean lab equipped with microscopes, lasers, and workshop tables. Visitors create digital mood boards, then work with the experts to polish and set stones. More unorthodox still, the company offers live-streamed footage of the jewelry-making process for friends and family unable to attend the appointment.

Korean eyewear brand Yun's Berlin flagship similarly capitalizes on the three-pronged allure of customization, transparency, and more than a little artfully engineered theatricality. The store features a state-of-the-art robotic machine that finishes lenses while customers watch, fitting precise prescriptions in just 20 minutes. Timewise, it's a lunch-break sweet spot also acknowledged by Canadian lip care brand Bite Beauty; its Toronto boutique invites visitors to co-create their own lipstick (color, finish, and flavor) with a beauty specialist, watching the magic of concocting the result while they wait.

Innovation in the landscape of reactionary retailing is best observed in Adidas's 2017 Knit for You Berlin pop-up. Part creative studio, part high-tech manufacturing lab, visitors could co-design and produce a sweater in under four hours. Significantly, the process centered around a QR code-enabled booklet that digitally stored details of each stage of the performance, a brand process that included stepping into a darkened room to discern patterns via gestural tech, color-switching RFID tools, and state-of-the-art body scanning. Masterfully revealing Adidas's drive to react faster to fashion trends, the concept is likely to trigger more spaces in which the final layer of design, bolstered by bearing witness to the inspiring processes, becomes a consumer privilege.

Promising personal expression, professional self-sharpening, and an edifying sense of cultural congress to a consumer in return for grassroots insights, "innovation boutiques" not only define a lucrative new world of fan-brand blended retailing but also prove their capacity to react to cultural seismic shifts at digital-era speed. In a time where transformation is key, and where the public increasingly demands their presence be felt in any given retail setting, these ventures define an elaborate set of tactics with which brands can remain relevant. <

AIRBNB Yoshino Cedar House

From the originators of the online rental accommodation business Airbnb comes a concept that seeks to reinvigorate dwindling rural communities via a house-building project, involving members of these communities from beginning to end.

Beautifully crafted and built exclusively from cedar wood, the Yoshino Cedar House was displayed at the House Vision exhibition in Tokyo, an event organized by Kenya Hara, the art director at Muji. The project considers the ways in which we might live in the future. A collaboration between Go Hasegawa, a Tokyo-based architect, and the founders of Airbnb, the house explores the relationships between such a structure, the people who build it, and those who will eventually stay in it; the house is now rented out as an Airbnb accommodation by the same community that built it. The inside is exquisite, crafted entirely from locally sourced timber. It is a showcase for the diverse range of applications of wood in a domestic environment, wood being infinitely more environmentally friendly than many other materials used in building. The walls, floors, and ceilings are all made from planks of cedar, as are the tables, chairs, and kitchen units. The effect is to give the home an overwhelming sense of harmony, even purity. <

LINDA FARROW Flagship Store

With an interior that juxtaposes rough plaster with glossy marble and polished concrete with brushed brass, STUDIO GIANCARLO VALLE blurs the lines between casual and refined to create a soft, calming backdrop for Linda Farrow's iconic sunglasses.

Established in 1970, Linda Farrow is the go-to label for vintage-inspired designer sunglasses. For their first New York store in SoHo, the company commissioned local firm Studio Giancarlo Valle, who was quick to pick up on the brand's iconic earthy luxury. Sandwiched between a concrete-tiled floor and a rough plaster ceiling, Linda Farrow wares are displayed on beautifully polished stands made of pink onyx and brushed brass. On one wall, little glazed boxes with brass trim display sunglasses pair by pair. Separate areas of the collection are defined by marble walls framing the retail space, one in natural honey tones, the other in a smoky gray. Bringing the two elements together—the rough with the smooth, the casual with the refined—the main display resembles abandoned concrete beams. Yet, as you look closer, the hollowed-out structures reveal a soft suede interior that delicately embraces the coveted eyewear collection. <

ACE & TATE Shop

Through collaborations with young, innovative design teams, the eyewear specilalists Ace & Tate have developed a brand identity that is truly planted in the twenty-first century. High-tech display stands and a sparing use of solid block color are common themes.

Conscious of the often prohibitive prices attached to designer glasses these days, and keen to establish a young client base that is likely to stay loyal for decades, Ace & Tate pride themselves on selling attractive, quality spectacles at a fair price. In order to lure bright young customers to their stores in the first place, the company kits out its showrooms with a fresh, contemporary vibe. Key to their designs is the need to maximize on the multifunctional nature of their business. Alongside large, clear, freestanding displays that allow customers to choose from the widest possible selection of frames, their interiors also incorporate smaller, private spaces in which consultations can take place. There is a brand focus on using the latest technological innovations to create state-of-the-art display stands. And, being patrons of the arts—Ace & Tate fund grants to emerging artists—the success of their store designs frequently lies in their bold use of color and a degree of whimsical flair. <

THE NEW STAND Mobile Retail Concept

The New Stand collaborated with Brooklyn-based UM PROJECT to push the mobile retail experience to a new level. With a modular shelf system that can be stacked in various ways to accommodate all kinds of merchandise, the underground stores seamlessly merge physical and online retail.

A play on the word "newsstand," this quirky New York retailer is a far cry from the typical street vendors stacked up with newspapers and magazines. The New Stand occupies small, brightly lit shops in NYC's subway stations and sells everything from coffee to funky toys and new media. So far, UM Project has created four playful, engaging, and flexible environments for The New Stand. Furniture, lighting, and fixtures are all integral to a design that centers on simple geometry, unpretentious materials, and a sparing use of bold color. Inspired by The New Stand app, and introducing innovative designs that include a multipurpose mobile cart, UM Project merges the physical with the virtual. Store furnishings almost look like 3-D renditions of computer software, where the various parts and pieces appear to be constantly in motion. Displays change on a daily basis, much to the delight of the brand's savvy clientele. <

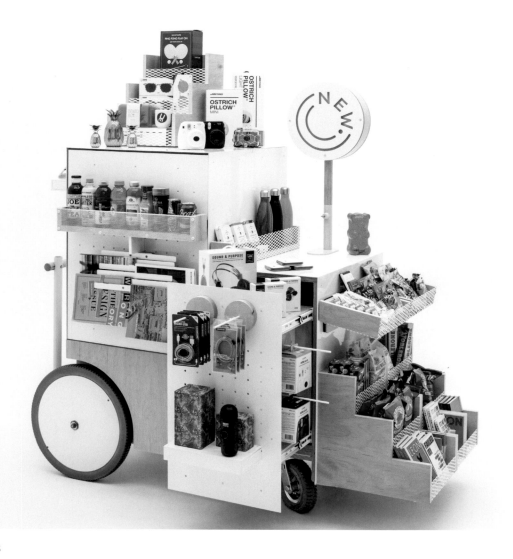

LA MELGUIZA Store

In a creation that suspends products in plexiglass boxes against a backdrop of honey-toned hues, ZOOCO ESTUDIO's intriguing design for La Melguiza in Madrid offers a whole-room visual representation of the exotic spice saffron.

When Zooco Estudio was asked to create the interior for a shop that would be entirely dedicated to saffron products, the designers came up with a retail concept that is inspired by the qualities of the spice. Its lightweight and delicate features have been translated in numerous jewel-like plexiglass boxes of different sizes that hang from the ceiling on delicate red filaments and display a sparkling light bulb or neatly packaged product. Set within smooth blond-wood walls, a series of amber-hued recesses display their wares. Here and there a simply framed photograph captures a scene from the harvest of the spice. The store façade is completely transparent. Peering through the glass, passersby catch a glimpse of the whole vision, as if looking into a box of saffron strands. The warmth and exoticism of saffron exudes from all corners of the store—in the honey-toned papers that line the recesses, the chestnut hue of the strip-wood ceiling, and the soft glow of the tungsten lamps. Just like saffron, the overall effect is at once precious and delicate. <

Across the depth of the store, red linear elements reminiscent of strands of saffron hang from the ceiling, suspending transparent boxes that are filled alternately with lights or the store's products.

CARIN Flagship Store

When designing the interior for Carin's flagship store in Seoul, Niiiz Design LAB created a laboratory-inspired environment for the ladies' sunglasses brand and softened the harsh edges of the interior elements with lush botanicals.

Introducing natural elements, specifically plants, into retail spaces is currently in vogue and South Korea's Niiiz Design LAB has coined a term for it: planterior. For the design of Carin's sunglasses showroom, they interpreted the genre by creating a minimalist laboratory-style backdrop and filling the spacious showroom with plant displays featuring sculptural succulents, cacti, and palms. The botanical design was created in collaboration with a florist, and the combination of green and white creates a fresh aesthetic and upbeat energy. In the window, Clarin's elegant wares are displayed in terrarium-style display cases on metal shelving units set against white-tiled walls. Located in Seoul's hip Hongdae neighborhood, the store's juxtaposition of nature and clean design hits just the right note with the target customer: the fashion-conscious yet eco-aware woman. <

INDEX

Museum of Supernatural History, Maison Shanghai
2015
Pages 146–147
Shanghai, China
Winbows by Zim & Zou
zimandzou.fr
France
Photography: Zim & Zou

The Fox's Den, Barcelona
Paseo de Gracia store
2014
Pages 148 (top) and 149
Barcelona, Spain
Winbows by Zim & Zou
zimandzou.fr
France
Photography: Nacho Vaquero

Forest Folks, Dubai,
Mall of the Emirates
2017
Pages 148 (bottom)
Dubai, U. A. E.
Winbows by Zim & Zou
zimandzou.fr
France
Photography: Zim & Zou

Contraptions,
London Bond Street store
2017
Pages 150–151
London, United Kingdom
Windows by Storey Studio
storeystudio.com
United Kingdom
Photography:
Francisco Ibáñez

Hermès Cats, Stockholm
store
2015
Page 152
Stockholm, Sweden
Window by Joann Tan Studio
joanntanstudio.com
Sweden
Photography: Patrik Lindell

Hermès Art, Stockholm store
2013
Page 153
Stockholm, Sweden
Window by Joann Tan Studio
joanntanstudio.com
Sweden
Photography: Patrik Lindell

The City Awakens,
Stockholm store
2015
Pages 154–155
Stockholm, Sweden
Windows by Joann Tan Studio
joanntanstudio.com
Sweden
Photography: Patrik Lindell

Jardan
jardan.com.au
Jardan Flagship Store
Sydney, Australia
　IF Architecture
　ifarchitecture.com.au
　Australia
　Photography: Sean Fennessy
　Pages 118–121

KaDeWe
kadewe.de
KaDeWe women's floor
Berlin, Germany
　India Mahdavi
　india-mahdavi.com
　France
　Pages 22–23

Kindo
Kindo Kid's Boutique
Monterrey, Mexico
　Anagrama
　anagrama.com
　Mexico
　Photography: Caroga Foto
　Pages 198–201

Krug
krug.com
The Krug Room at the
Mandarin Oriental Hotel
Hong Kong, China
　Substance
　aworkofsubstance.com
　Hong Kong
　Photography: Dennis Lo
　Pages 72–73

L'Échoppe
lechoppe.jp
L'Échoppe concept store
Tokyo, Japan
　CUT Architectures
　cut-architectures.com
　France
　Photography: David Foessel
　Pages 210–211

La Melguiza
lamelguiza.es
La Melguiza Store
Madrid, Spain
　Zooco Estudio
　zooco.es
　Photography: Imagen
　Subliminal
　Pages 248–249

Linda Farrow
int.lindafarrow.com
Linda Farrow Flagship Store
New York, United States
　Giancarlo Valle
　giancarlovalle.com
　United States
　Photography: Brooke Holm
　Pages 242–243

Max & Co.
world.maxandco.com
Minimal Terrarium windows
Milan, Italy
　Studiopepe
　studiopepe.info
　Italy
　Photography: Silvia Rivoltella
　Pages 76–77

Moelcure Pharmacy
Moelcure Pharmacy
Taichung, Taiwan
　Waterfrom Design
　waterfrom.com
　Taiwan
　Photography: Kuomin Lee
　Pages 62–63

Nike
nike.com
United States
Pages 220–237

　Nike GC Air Max Day 2016
　Pages 220–223
　Hong Kong, China
　Rosie Lee
　rosielee.co.uk
　United Kingdom
　Photography:
　Nike Brand Design

　Pigalle Basketball Court
　Pages 224–225
　Paris, France
　Ill Studio
　ill-studio.com
　France
　Photography: Lionel Mokuba

　Nike Opening Finals 2017
　Pages 226–227
　Portland, Oregon, United
　States
　Storey Studio
　storeystudio.com
　United Kingdom
　Photography: Dina Avila

　Nike GC Air Max Day 2017
　Pages 228–229
　Shanghai, China
　Rosie Lee
　rosielee.co.uk
　United Kingdom
　Photography:
　Nike Brand Design

　Nike Sole DXB
　Pages 230–231
　Dubai, U. A. E.
　Rosie Lee
　rosielee.co.uk
　United Kingdom
　Photography:
　Nike Brand Design

　Nike GC CR7 Tour
　Pages 232–233
　Shanghai, China
　Rosie Lee
　rosielee.co.uk
　United Kingdom
　Photography:
　Nike Brand Design

SHOPLIFTER!

New Retail Architecture
and Brand Spaces

This book was conceived, edited, and designed by Gestalten.

Edited by Robert Klanten and Anja Kouznetsova

Preface by Alison Embrey Medina

Brand case studies by Clara Le Fort (Fendi, pp. 84–89; and Hermès, pp. 136–155)
with special thanks to Cyril Feb for his assistance on the Hermès case study;
and Anna Sinofzik (Architecture at Large, pp. 42–51; Gentle Monster, pp. 166–189;
and Siam Discovery, pp. 104–115);

Store descriptions and captions by Anna Southgate

Essays by Katie Baron (The Rise of the Innovation Boutique, pp. 238–239),
Doron Beuns (Luxury Brand Narratives and Architecture, pp. 116–117).
Alison Embrey Medina (Retail's Future is Physical, pp. 24–27;
and The Permanent Impermanence of Pop-Up Retail, pp. 38–41),
Katharina Michalski (Brand Utility, pp. 205–209; Experiential Retail, pp. 64–67;
and From Concept Store to Lifestyle Retail, pp. 164–165),
and Anna Sinofzik (Olfactive Branding, pp. 100–103)

Illustrations by Eleni Debo

Project Management by Adam Jackman

Creative Direction of Design by Ludwig Wendt
Layout by Ludwig Wendt and Stefan Morgner

Typeface: Calibre by Kris Sowersby, Klim Type Foundry

Printed by Nino Druck GmbH, Neustadt/Weinstraße
Made in Germany

Published by Gestalten, Berlin 2018
ISBN 978-3-89955-941-5

Bibliographic information published by the Deutsche Nationalbibliothek.
The Deutsche Nationalbibliothek lists this publication in the Deutsche Nationalbibliografie;
detailed bibliographic data are available online at
http://dnb.d-nb.de.

None of the content in this book was published in exchange
for payment by commercial parties or designers;
Gestalten selected all included work based solely on its artistic merit.

This book was printed on paper certified according
to the standards of the FSC®.

MIX
Paper from
responsible sources
FSC® C006655
FSC
www.fsc.org